CUSTER'S GOLD

CUSTER'S GOLD

THE UNITED STATES CAVALRY EXPEDITION

OF 1874

by Donald Jackson

UNIVERSITY OF NEBRASKA PRESS
LINCOLN AND LONDON

Preface

PREFACE

If a book has George Armstrong Custer in it, the Custer personality takes over nearly every page. But this is not a Custer book in the larger sense, for the battle it describes is more significant than the skirmish on the Little Big Horn that cost Custer his life. The battle for the continent, which white men waged with the Indians for three centuries, is typified in the contest for the Black Hills. "We have always observed," said the New York *Times* in 1874, "that when white men want a reservation, it is at once discovered that the Indians have no honest use for it." To examine that characteristic of the American people, as reflected in the taking of the Black Hills, is the main purpose of this book. A second purpose is to portray an army expedition in detail —the routines of life in camp and on the road which we can best recover from sources such as Private Theodore Ewert's journal and the reports of the newspaper correspondents.

In referring to officers I have used brevet rank, except where actual rank appears in quoted passages. Although an officer's actual rank was nearly always used in official correspondence, his brevet rank was employed as a matter of courtesy in social and informal usage, and I have found it convenient to retain the custom. The War Department knew Custer as a lieutenant colonel; the world knew him as Brevet Major General George Armstrong Custer, and so he remains in the pages which follow.

I am grateful to Mrs. Melma Huckeby Ewert, of Jacksonville, Illinois, for permission to use the Theodore Ewert journal, and to the Yale University Library for permission to quote from Custer's order and dispatch book. I have been

helped particularly by Miss Doris Probst, Miss Alma De-
Jordy, and other staff members of the University of Illinois
Library; Miss Margaret Rose, of the State Historical Society
of North Dakota; Mr. Willoughby M. Babcock, of the
Minnesota Historical Society; Mr. Don Rickey, Jr., formerly
of the Custer Battlefield National Monument; Mr. George E.
Hyde, of Omaha, Nebraska; and many helpful staff members of the National Archives and the Library of Congress,
in Washington, D.C. Photographs by Illingworth are repro-
duced from a set of stereographs in the National Archives,
except Fig. 12, which is from the State Historical Society of
South Dakota. Maps are by Herbert L. Sterrett, of the University of Illinois Press.

The Research Board of the University of Illinois has
generously supported my work.

D. J.

Urbana, Illinois
1966

Contents

Illustrations

Abbreviations

These abbreviations are used frequently in the footnotes:

AGO   Adjutant General's office
GPO   Government Printing Office
LR   Letters received
LS   Letters sent
NA   National Archives
RG   Record group in the National Archives

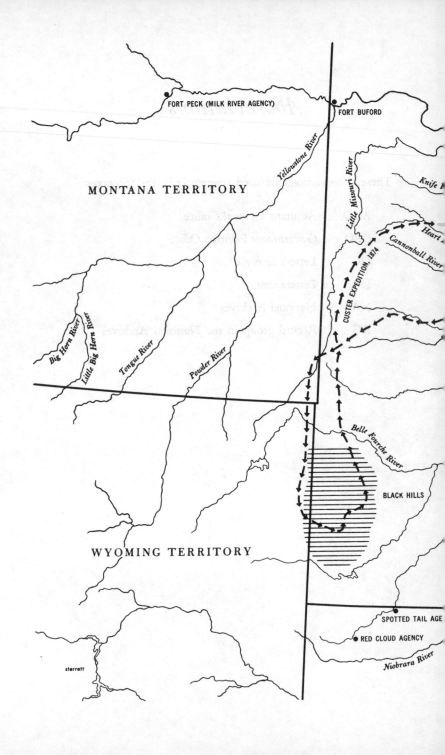

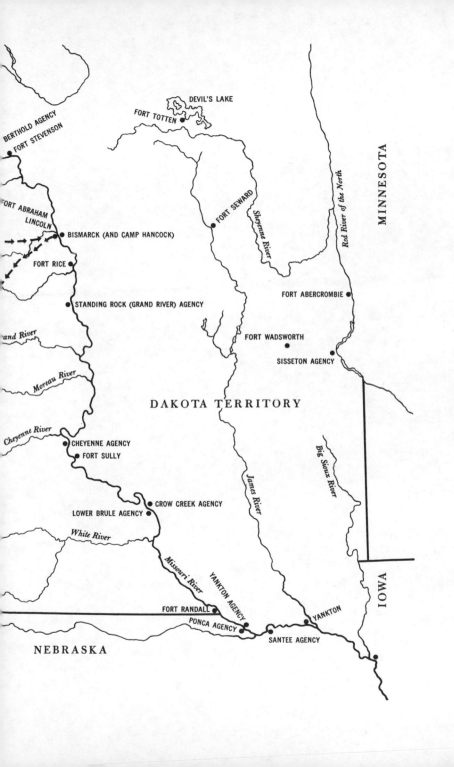

CHAPTER 1

Away to the Black Hills

July 2, 1874

The arc of prairie, the line between Dakota earth and sky, was blurred by the skimmering little flights of a great many grasshoppers. Over the hilltop came a single rider whose horse brought up new clusters of the swarming insects as its hooves swept through the scant turf of grama grass. The sunburnt face of the man, and his moustache the color of new hemp rope, were known the nation over. All his trappings were legend: the buckskin shirt, the gray felt hat, the red kerchief showing at his throat, the staghounds and foxhounds that ran with him, and the rosewood bay horse that never tired.

As the soldier and his mount descended the hill, a scattering of mounted men appeared behind him. Then the waggling ears and bobbing heads of the army mules broke across the horizon, and the white fabric tops of the wagons billowed up like a rising cloud. Soon the hillside was covered with six-mule teams as the ponderous wagons came coasting down the incline. With the pressure gone from their traces, some of the mules broke into a trot, and the cursing of the teamsters as they hauled on the guide lines rang out in a harsh chorus.

The U.S. Cavalry expedition of 1874 was pounding a trail into the Dakota sod that would last for generations. In some places, sunflowers would take root in eight perfect rows to mark the furrows which the wheels were making. But even after the wind and rain of decades had smoothed the ruts, the real line that Major General George A. Custer was drawing would still be there. It was an indelible line between white man and red man.

In the eyes of the Army the purpose of the expedition was to reconnoiter an unknown patch of the West called the Black Hills, along the Dakota–Wyoming border, where hostile bands of Teton Sioux had been withdrawing safely after raiding settlers on the plains of Nebraska. To the rest of the world, and more particularly to the residents of all the new little towns on the Missouri River who were aching to push westward, the purpose of the expedition was to look for gold. The discovery of gold—even on land legally held by the Sioux—could be expected to relieve some of the economic pressures created a year earlier by the Panic of 1873. Gold-hungry men along the frontier were ready to violate treaty terms and risk an Indian uprising by surging into the Black Hills—if Custer found gold.

A few white men had penetrated the Hills, some to be killed and some to return with fragmentary accounts of their journeys. In 1874 it still could be said that here was a very large stretch of *terra incognita*. Fur traders had skirted it for a century; old military trails crisscrossed at its perimeter; a flourishing civilization had crept to within two hundred miles. But of the Black Hills area itself the American people and their government knew almost nothing.[1]

    1. For the early history of the Black Hills, see George W. Kingsbury, *History of Dakota Territory*, published as the first two volumes of George Martin Smith, ed., *South Dakota, Its History and Its People*, 5 vols. (Chicago, 1915). See also Harold E. Briggs, "The Black Hills Gold Rush," *North Dakota Historical Quarterly*, 7 (1930–31), 71–99; and C. C. Oharra, "Custer's Black Hills Expedition of 1874," *Black Hills Engineer*, 17 (1929), 221 ff. For a more recent study of the area, see Herbert S. Schell, *History of South Dakota* (Lincoln, Nebr., 1961),

HISTORY OF A RUMOR

Probably the first white men to see the Hills were François and Louis-Joseph Verendrye, French explorers from the north who reportedly climbed Bear Butte in 1743 and viewed the blue-black slopes from a distance. Their Indian guides, fearing the hostile bands who dwelt among the Hills, would take them no farther.

Meriwether Lewis and William Clark heard French traders tell of the Hills during their journey up the Missouri in 1804. Wilson P. Hunt's expedition from St. Louis to the Pacific may have passed north of the Hills in 1811. In 1823, a band of about fifteen fur traders led by Jedediah Smith entered the southern hills and pushed on to the northwest, becoming the first party to leave a record of its passage.

Soon the prospecting began. Ezra Kind and six companions went up from Laramie in 1833, stayed a year, found gold, and perished. When all had died but Kind, he scraped a record on a slab of buff sandstone: "Got all of the gold we could carry our ponys all got by the Indians I have lost my gun and nothing to eat and Indians hunting me." It was a sort of epitaph.

In the summer of 1852 a prospecting party of thirty men broke off from an expedition bound for California and went gold-hunting in the Hills. Eight men came out and reported gold; the rest were never heard of again. Like many other reports of travel in the Hills, this one must be viewed with skepticism, for the term "Black Hills" in those days could also apply to the Laramie Range along the North Platte in Wyoming, much nearer the old emigrant trails. Also in

and for an extensive bibliography of works dealing with the Black Hills, see J. Leonard Jennewein, *Black Hills Booktrails* (Mitchell, S.D., 1962).

1852, scientific exploration of the region began as Dr. John Evans, with the David Dale Owens geological survey, mapped the badlands and the eastern foothills.

Army men felt that the area was bound to cause trouble, either as a rallying point for raiding Indians or a dangerous El Dorado for gold seekers. Military commanders in the 1850s had no desire to enter the region and risk a war with the Sioux, but at times their assignments brought them dangerously close. Brigadier General William S. Harney was sent from Fort Leavenworth in 1855 on a punitive expedition against the Indians. He won a vastly one-sided battle with the Brules at Ash Hollow in Nebraska, went on to Fort Laramie, then headed for Fort Pierre (at the site of present Pierre, South Dakota) by way of the head of the White River. This took him through the lower edge of the Hills country and gave his geologist, Dr. Ferdinand V. Hayden, a chance to make some observations in the White River badlands. Two years later Harney's topographical engineer, Lieutenant G. K. Warren, came close to a penetration of the Hills while reconnoitering, but he was turned back at the Wyoming–Dakota line at the insistence of Hunkpapa and Miniconjou bands. In 1859, Captain W. F. Raynolds (with Dr. Hayden) led an expedition from Fort Pierre toward the upper end of the Hills, but veered north into Wyoming and the Yellowstone country of Montana.

Both east and west margins of the Hills were reconnoitered in 1865 by elements of the unlucky Powder River expedition which, much handicapped by poor planning, bad weather, and improper food, marched from Fort Laramie to the Panther Mountains on the Tongue River.

Yearning for Black Hills gold now began in an organized manner. Probably the first citizens' group was the Black Hills Exploring and Mining Association formed in Yankton, Dakota Territory, in January 1861. Several meetings were

held early in the year and the membership grew to include
about half the men in Yankton, but not much was accom-
plished. The Civil War occupied the minds of men during
the following years, and Sioux uprisings in Minnesota made
the miners wary; but in January 1865 the Association was
back in business. The group issued a broadside that spring,
printed in the office of the Yankton *Union and Dakotaian,*
promoting a "new and short route" to the gold mines of the
Black Hills, Montana, and Idaho. The route passed through
Sioux City, Iowa, and Yankton, then continued in a nearly
direct line to the Hills.

The Legislative Assembly of Dakota Territory approved
a memorial to Congress in December 1865, asking for a
geological survey of the Hills. Introduced by Moses K.
Armstrong, one of the charter members of the mining group
in Yankton, it suggested that the survey be carried out in
cooperation with military forces of the territory under
Brigadier General Alfred Sully. When the Assembly also
memorialized the Secretary of War on the establishment of
a military post on the north base of the Hills, this comment
came from Major General John Pope: "It is my purpose
as soon as the season opens to place as large a military post
as the force at my command enables me to do, on or near
the upper waters of the Big Cheyenne, at the northern base
of the Black Hills, with a view to open that country to explorers, and to constitute one of the posts on the route via
Powder River and the Big Horn Mountains, to Montana.
The post will be established as early as practicable in the
spring."[2]

No post was established and no military escort for miners
appeared, but the citizens of the Missouri River towns kept
on hoping. Dr. Hayden renewed their enthusiasm October 6,

2. Quoted in Kingsbury, *1*:865–66.

1866, when he addressed a meeting in Yankton presided over by Governor Andrew J. Faulk. Yes, he said, there was a strong possibility of rich deposits in the Hills. His travels with Lieutenant Warren and Captain Raynolds had persuaded him of it.

Since the Army had never really refused protection to a party of miners, and since Dr. Hayden was a man whose opinion about minerals bore weight, the Black Hills Exploring and Mining Association came alive again. Another broadside appeared, proposing an expedition that would start about June 15 for the gold fields. "Very many of the scientific institutions of the country will be represented, and expect to accompany the expedition, which will make the enterprise not only a profitable but an interesting one, to all who join it."

It was apparent by now that someone in the War Department had let the organizers believe that a military escort would be provided. The man who must authorize this escort, however, was General William T. Sherman, commanding the Military Division of Missouri from St. Louis. He not only withheld protection but also forbade the expedition to move, in a letter of May 27, 1867, to General Alfred Terry: "I agree with you perfectly that we are not in a position to permit an invasion of that region, for no sooner would a settlement be inaugurated, than an appeal would come for protection. . . . You may, therefore, forbid all white people going there at present, and warn all who go in spite of your prohibition, that the United States will not protect them now, or until public notice is given that the Indian title is extinguished."[3]

Not everyone believed that the Army could or would ban travel to the Hills. In the fall of 1867 Captain P. B. Davy,

3. Kingsbury, 1:863.

of Blue Earth City, Minnesota, arrived in Yankton and began to organize an expedition that would move out the next spring. He had signed up about three hundred men when the Army stepped in, instructing General D. S. Stanley, commanding the district of southeast Dakota from Fort Sully, to use force if necessary to stop Davy.

Then Davy was stopped, the Black Hills Exploring and Mining Association was stopped, and the gaudy dreams of every frontiersman were interrupted by a treaty designed to bring peace to all the central West.

THE TREATY OF 1868 AND ITS EFFECTS

In an atmosphere of doubt and mistrust, the United States negotiated a treaty with the Plains tribes in 1868. Its authors hoped it would end a twenty-five-year span of raids and retaliations, of promises made and forgotten, and of costly trial and error by the government. Planning now to introduce a benevolent policy that would win the Indian over, the government surrendered a great deal to the Sioux, Cheyenne, and Arapaho tribes. The Bozeman trail to the Montana gold fields was to be closed and Forts Phil Kearny, C. F. Smith, and Reno evacuated. The Sioux were to be given a reservation consisting of that part of Dakota Territory lying west of the Missouri. Generous annuities were provided for a few years, and there would be education for Indian children and agricultural instruction for the men.

In return, the Indians promised not to molest the builders of the Union Pacific, then inching a track across the Plains. They also blandly agreed not to bother wagon trains, and not to scalp white men or capture their women and children.

One of the provisions of the treaty which would prove most troublesome was the exclusion of white men from the Sioux reservation. The government agreed "that no persons except those herein designated and authorized so to do, and except such officers, agents, and employes of the government as may be authorized to enter upon Indian reservations in discharge of duties enjoined by law, shall ever be permitted to pass over, settle upon, or reside in the territory described in this article."[4]

So the pressure of westward movement toward the Black Hills was halted for a time. The novelty of comparatively peaceful days on the frontier, and the realization that the Army planned to enforce the treaty terms, kept the gold fever quiescent for two or three years—but the settlers cherished every small anecdote that renewed the old promise. Tempting information came from men of probity and reputation. Father Pierre Jean De Smet, a respected Jesuit missionary, told editor Charles Collins in Sioux City that he believed there were valuable mineral deposits in the Hills. And Governor John A. Burbank related that while he had been an agent at the Red Cloud agency he had received a piece of ore from the badlands on the White River which, when assayed, contained an equivalent of $109.74 per ton of silver.

A new tone came into the street-corner talk and the newspaper comment along the Missouri. From a typical editorial in the Yankton *Press and Dakotaian:*

> This abominable compact with the marauding bands that regularly make war on the whites in the summer and live on government bounty all winter, is now pleaded as a barrier to the improvement and development of one of the richest and most fertile sections in America. What shall be done with these Indian dogs in our manger? They will not dig the gold or let others

4. See complete text of the treaty in Appendix 2, pp. 127–36.

do it. . . . They are too lazy and too much like mere animals to cultivate the fertile soil, mine the coal, develop the salt mines, bore the petroleum wells, or wash the gold. Having all these things in their hands, they prefer to live as paupers, thieves and beggars; fighting, torturing, hunting, gorging, yelling and dancing all night to the beating of old tin kettles. . . . Anyone who knows how utterly they depend on the government for subsistence will see that if they have to be supported at all, they might far better occupy small reservations and be within military reach, than to have the exclusive control of a tract of country as large as the whole State of Pennsylvania or New York, which they can neither improve or utilize.[5]

Charles Collins, editor of the Sioux City *Times,* became an active leader of the move to invade the Hills in the early 1870s, and he had plenty of followers. Exploring parties were forming as far east as Massachusetts. Prominent citizens of Yankton, such as Judge W. W. Brookings, seemed even more excited than they had been in 1866. Judge Brookings told a meeting in March 1872, "There are other sources of wealth in the Black Hills besides the gold. We want the lumber to build our cities and towns, and the fact that there is an abundance of pine there will be an additional inducement to stimulate the enterprise."[6] Congressman Moses K. Armstrong introduced a bill to provide for the purchase of the Black Hills pinelands from the Sioux. If the Indians refused to sell, the Secretary of War would be authorized to

5. Yankton *Press and Dakotaian,* Sept. 3, 1874. Though written immediately after the expedition, the extract is typical of the attitude during all the early 1870s.

6. Yankton *Press,* March 13, 1872; the word *Dakotaian* had not yet been added to the masthead.

negotiate with them for the right to erect sawmills and send lumber down to the prairie regions by raft.[7]

There was rivalry between Sioux City and Yankton over the best route to the Hills. Sioux City was promoting the "Sawyer's Road," a wagon trail which missed Yankton. The route recommended by Yankton residents ran along the north shore of the Missouri and passed through their town. Merchants in both places needed the trade that migrant gold hunters would bring them.

Columbus Delano, the Secretary of the Interior, warned Governor Burbank in March 1872 that the President had requested "a stop to be put" to the latest Black Hills movement. It became necessary in April for Edwin Stanton McCook, secretary of Dakota Territory, to issue a proclamation warning against combinations of men which "have been and are now being made with a view to entering . . . the region . . . under the plea that the said Black Hills country has valuable mineral deposits."

At the same time, the Army cracked down again. Editor Collins received a letter from General Alfred Terry, in command of the Department of Dakota with headquarters in St. Paul, Minnesota, reminding Collins' readers of the Treaty of 1868. Terry said that any parties organized for the purpose of visiting or prospecting in the Hills would be engaging in an unlawful enterprise, "the consummation of which it will be my duty, under the law, and my instructions, to prevent, by the use, if necessary, of the troops at my disposal."[8]

Considering the times and the temper of western men, both white and red, the assurances which the Sioux had given the treaty commissioners in 1868 were meaningless. The Indians had said they would never attack any person,

7. Ibid., March 20, 1872.
8. Ibid., April 10, 1872.

"at home, nor travelling," would never scalp white men or
capture their women and children. Even if Red Cloud and
other signatories had vowed in deadly earnestness to observe
these un-Indian terms, they never could have enforced them.
The tribes were too scattered, the young men too hot-
blooded, and thousands of warriors did not recognize or
even understand the treaty.

The famous "peace policy" of President Ulysses S. Grant,
who took office in 1869, was in full operation. The policy
consisted of these aims: First, to get the Indians onto reservations as soon as possible, "where they can be provided for
in such manner as the dictates of humanity and Christian
civilization require." Second, to treat with severity any tribe
or band that refuses to go on a reservation. Third, to provide
all supplies at fair prices, guarding against graft and specula-
tion. Fourth, to cooperate with religious organizations to
procure competent religious agents to care for the reservation Indians and handle the distribution of goods. Fifth, to
work with religious organizatons in the establishment of
schools and churches.[9]

The operation of Grant's policy, and years of contact with
white westerners, had gradually divided the Plains Indians
into three categories: wild, undecided, and subdued. There
were Sioux in all these groups, and indeed no other Indians
were nearly so important during this period on the Northern
Plains. The great division called the Teton Sioux consisted
of several groups—the upper and lower Brules, the Oglalas,
Miniconjous, Sans Arcs, Two Kettles, Hunkpapas, and
Blackfoot-Sioux.

Most of the dangerous Sioux bands lived between the
100th and 111th meridians and ranged from the Canadian
line to the Wyoming country. They included the fierce,

9. Delano's letter of April 15 to the *Times* is reprinted in the Yankton *Press*, April 30, 1872.

demonstrative Hunkpapas under Sitting Bull, plus some
Miniconjous, Sans Arcs, Oglalas, and probably unregenerate
elements from all the Teton Sioux. Some of them were wily
enough to report in to the Milk River Agency at Fort Peck
for supplies without getting involved with civilization, and
others trailed down through the Black Hills to winter with
Red Cloud and Spotted Tail. Still others, at least four
hundred lodges by one estimate, had never visited any agency
and wanted no part of the white man's flour and beef.

Although he could not speak for the wide-ranging warriors of the North, the Oglala chief named Red Cloud was
the acknowledged spokesman for nearly all the Teton Sioux.
When the treaty was signed he brought his band to an
agency, first in Wyoming Territory along the Platte and
then in northwestern Nebraska. Not far away was the
agency of Spotted Tail and his Upper Brules. Both these
chiefs thought they were settling on the new Sioux reservation in Dakota Territory, but when the northern boundary
line of Nebraska was run in the summer of 1874, these
agencies proved to be south of the line.

Although Red Cloud and Spotted Tail were at peace with
the whites, their activities were closely watched by the Army
and the settlers. Young braves could be influenced by the
winter visitors from the wild northern bands. One report
said that at least half the men had Spencer or Winchester
rifles, the rest had single-shot breechloaders, and that it was
possible for one Indian to have as many as three thousand
rounds of ammunition; but white men invariably over-
estimated the number of modern weapons owned by Indians.

About 6,500 Sioux and many other Plains Indians had
submitted to the demands of the government and had undertaken a new way of life. Their agencies were scattered from
Montana Territory to Nebraska and they were poor or pros-
perous, docile or restless, Christian or heathen, depending

on circumstances. In the Wind River Valley of Wyoming
Territory were the Eastern Shoshonis, who had to be pro-
tected from the Northern Cheyennes and Arapahoes by
U.S. troops. Up in Montana Territory were the Flatheads,
Blackfeet, Bloods, Piegans, Mountain and River Crows,
Gros Ventres, Assiniboines, and some Northern Crees from
Canada. In eastern Dakota were several establishments for
the Sioux, including Devil's Lake Agency, Lake Traverse
Agency, Cheyenne River Agency, Grand River Agency,
Upper Sioux or Crow Creek Agency, Lower Brule Agency,
and Yankton Agency. There were Arikaras, Gros Ventres,
and Mandans at Fort Berthold, and Poncas at Fort Randall.
Just across the line in northeastern Nebraska were the
Santees who, with the Sissetons and Wahpetons in eastern
Dakota, were classified as Eastern Sioux.[10]

The Army's Decision

All the wild Indians and most of the "tame" ones listed
above lived in the military area called the Department of
Dakota, embracing the territories of Montana and Dakota
and the state of Minnesota. The commander, Brigadier
General Alfred Terry in St. Paul, was responsible to the
commander of the Division of Missouri. The division commander was Lieutenant General Philip H. Sheridan, whose
superiors in Washington included General William T.

10. The location and disposition of the tribes is based upon the
*Annual Report of the Commissioner of Indian Affairs . . . for the Year
1874* (Washington, GPO, 1874); an analysis in John W. Smith to
George A. Custer, Feb. 25, 1874, Fort Abraham Lincoln, LS, RG 98,
NA; and a report of annual inspection of the military posts in the
Department of Dakota by Lt. Col. E. S. Otis, Nov. 10, 1875, Dept. of
Dakota, LR, No. 285 (1876), RG 98, NA. For a thorough study of the
Indian problem in the region, see James C. Olson, *Red Cloud and the
Sioux Problem* (Lincoln, Nebr., 1965).

Sherman, the Commanding General of the Army, and
W. W. Belknap, the Secretary of War. When the Sioux
committed violence against western settlers, one of these
four men inevitably got his name in the paper, and in 1873
and 1874 this happened regularly.

Because the amount of exposed frontier in the Department of Dakota was small, the hostiles looked south to
Nebraska for settlers to plunder. This meant that Indians
under General Terry's supervision were slipping down into
the Department of the Platte, commanded by Brigadier
General E. O. C. Ord. They were Terry's Indians, but he had
no way to stop them from raiding in Ord's area. He needed
a post in the Black Hills region.

Sheridan summed it up in his annual report for 1874:

> In order to better control the Indians making these
> raids toward the south, I had contemplated, for two or
> three years past, to establish a military post in the coun-
> try known as the Black Hills, and in my last annual
> report, recommended the establishment of a large post
> there, so that by holding an interior point in the heart
> of the Indian country we could threaten the villages
> and stock of the Indians, if they made raids on our
> settlements. With this view I mentioned the subject in
> the presence of the President, the honorable Secretary
> of the Interior, the honorable Secretary of War, and
> the General of the Army, last fall, and meeting with a
> favorable response from the Secretary of the Interior,
> who has exclusive charge of Indian affairs, I set to work
> to make a reconnaissance of the country about which
> dreamy stories have been told, especially by Father De
> Smet.
>   I first thought that Fort Laramie, which is not much
> more than one hundred miles from the Black Hills,

would be the best place to start the reconnaissance from, but on visiting Fort Laramie last fall, and again in the winter, I found the condition of the temper of the Indians such as would probably provoke hostilities. I then turned my attention to Fort A. Lincoln, on the Missouri River, at the end of the Northern Pacific Railroad, where most of the Seventh Cavalry, under command of Lieut. Col. George A. Custer was stationed, as the most suitable place to start from, although the distance was three times as great as from Fort Laramie. On visiting Fort Lincoln in the spring, I found everything favorable. . . . I then returned and secured the necessary authority for the reconnaissance, and directed General Terry to organize the expedition and put Colonel Custer in command, whom I thought especially fitted for such an undertaking.[11]

INTO CAMP AND ONTO THE ROAD

After visiting Fort Lincoln in the spring of 1874, Sheridan started the paperwork. He wrote Sherman on May 1 that he was ready to authorize the expedition, and Sherman approved it. Two weeks later, Sheridan's adjutant instructed General Terry to send a column of nine or ten companies of the Seventh Cavalry, under the command of Custer, to examine the country in and about the north fork of the Cheyenne, the country south of it in the vicinity of Bear Butte, and especially the area south and west of the Butte which was commonly designated as the Black Hills.[12]

Terry's special order No. 117, of June 8, giving Custer

11. *Message From the President to the Two Houses of Congress . . .* (Washington, GPO, 1874), p. 410.
12. Chicago *Inter-Ocean,* Aug. 28, 1874.

his direct authorization, was released to the newspapers.[13] The residents of the Missouri River towns figured the Army had finally come to its senses; Custer was going to find the gold.

Fort Abraham Lincoln was a new post across the river from the roistering town of Bismarck. Unlike older fortifications, it had no log stockade with loopholed blockhouses at the corners; it was simply a collection of stables and barracks, the officers' houses on higher ground, no trees in sight but a few cottonwood whips being nursed along by the soldiers, and no drinking water but the gritty stuff dipped up from the Missouri.

Twenty-five miles down the river was Fort Rice, an older post established in 1864, rebuilt in 1868, and protected by a stockade of gray cottonwood logs. Four companies of the Seventh Cavalry were here, commanded by Lieutenant Colonel Joseph G. Tilford. Tilford's ill health, temperament, and ways of command provoked Custer to sarcastic impatience. The two men despised one another vigorously.

Terry's special order had placed Custer in command of both posts and had pitched the garrisons into a program of strenuous activity. Only a month to get ready, and every day of it needed. Custer required mules, supplies, teamsters, and recruits which the War Department would not give him. He asked for 150 new men to fill out his company rosters, and was refused. The prospect for officers of field grade was also poor; Major Marcus Reno was up on the Canadian border with D and I companies, guarding the Northern Boundary Survey Commission, and Colonel Tilford would probably elect to stay in garrison.

On May 18, Custer issued a circular to his company commanders, instructing them to prepare their commands for the field without delay. Deficiencies in stores and equipment

13. It appeared in the *Press and Dakotaian,* July 2, 1874.

were to be reported. Morning drill was to be discontinued in favor of a heavy regimen of target practice. During the days that followed, the post adjutant issued dozens of circulars and special orders, and the Bismarck telegraph operator kept busy filing dispatches to Terry and Sheridan.

Custer asked Terry for two infantry companies to serve as guard for the wagon train. He liked the mobility of dismounted men around the wagons and he respected the firepower of their .50 caliber Springfields. Terry approved the request on condition that Custer could manage it without added expense, and assigned him Company G of the Seventeenth Infantry, from the Grand River Agency, and Company I of the Twentieth, from Fort Pembina at the far northern edge of the Territory.

For a daily ration of 3.5 pounds of forage per animal, the command would need more than 200,000 pounds of corn. Terry took steps to requisition it. Custer said he did not want mixed corn and oats, the common ration, as it took up too much wagon space. Even considering the cost of the corn, there would be a large saving in forage, for in garrison the daily ration was ten pounds of grain plus hay. With the horses and mules living mainly on grass, a saving of about $13,000 would be realized. Subtract from this the cost of hiring teamsters, and still the expedition would show a profit. Soldiers had to be fed whether on the march or in quarters. It was cheaper to go than stay.

To provide fresh meat, a herd of medium-weight steers was collected. Heavy cattle would have been worthless to a moving army; they soon grew footsore and laggard.

Now it began to appear that the command would not be ready to move on schedule. Custer wired Terry that he lacked weapons and his men badly needed more target practice; the lariats had not arrived; every day spent in preparation was worthwhile. During the training period, two hundred

Sioux from the Grand River Agency came up to protest the expedition. Small delegations kept coming in later, each time with a fat chief named Running Antelope as spokesman, and each time Custer explained his peaceful intentions. But the glower and mumble that resulted from his explanations made him cautious.[14]

Late in May the Indians diverted the energies of Custer and his men, disrupting the preparations for the trip. A party of four hundred Sioux left their Cheyenne River Agency with the obvious purpose of attacking their old enemies at Fort Berthold, the Arikaras and Mandans. Since the Cheyenne River Agency was below Forts Rice and Lincoln, and Fort Berthold was eighty miles higher up the river, it was necessary for Custer to try to intercept the war party as it crossed the plains west of his post. "The Rees [Arikaras] and Mandans should be protected the same as white settlers," wired Sheridan. Custer sent Colonel Tilford from Fort Rice with 160 mounted men to scout the tributaries of the Cannonball and try to learn whether the Indians had crossed. If they had, Custer meant to follow with his own troops. "I deem it of far more importance that a check should be given to this war party than the expedition should start promptly," he wired his superiors.

Tilford plodded forty miles to the west and came back, having found a stale moccasin track but no Indians. But this time Custer was suspecting that the Sioux had headed for the Bighorn and Yellowstone country to join the non-agency hostiles. But another scouting party came in to say that the Indians already had crossed the Heart going north. Custer took a detachment several miles up the Heart, ex-

14. The many details of preparing for the expedition are drawn from a collection of copies and extracts marked "Special Orders, General Orders, and Circulars from Headquarters, Black Hills Expedition, 1874," Fort Abraham Lincoln, RG 98, NA.

amined all the country between the Cannonball and the
Knife, and convinced himself there was not an Indian in the
area. He told Terry he supposed the tracks his men had
found along the Heart were from an observation party.
Anyway, he said, not much harm could be done now that
Fort Berthold had been alerted.

With a little more persistence and some of the proverbial
Custer luck, he would have found the four hundred Sioux.
They were doing just what their agent had said they were:
moving up to attack their traditional enemies at Berthold.
Instead of pressing the search farther, Custer abandoned it.
At seven o'clock on the morning of June 13 a small party
fired on the Arikaras and Mandans near the fort, luring
them into an ambuscade. Then all four hundred raiders
opened fire. Five Arikaras and a Mandan were killed and
badly mutilated, and the happy Sioux warriors returned to
their agency.[15]

Every time a Northern Pacific train pulled into the Bismarck station, the roster of military and civilian personnel
grew. Custer planned to divide his cavalry into two battalions
and give the right wing to Brigadier General George A.
Forsyth of the Ninth Cavalry, who was acting aide-de-camp
to Sheridan. At first Custer tried hard to get someone from
outside to take the left wing, but finally he had to settle for
Colonel Tilford. The colonel had been given the choice of
going or staying and had chosen to stay, but now he was
ordered up from Fort Rice with his detachment. His health
was bad (he had not gone to the Yellowstone the year before
for that reason), and obviously he did not relish the prospect
of the close-quarter hazing that Custer could give him in the
field.

15. Letters and telegrams dealing with the attack at Fort Berthold,
Fort Abraham Lincoln, LS, May 7, 1874, to June 28, 1877, pp. 77, 81,
83, 85, 114, and Department of Dakota, LS, 6, p. 108, RG 98, NA.

President Grant's son Frederick came from Chicago to serve as acting aide to Custer. It was a useless assignment and there is nothing to indicate that young Grant performed any vital service, but it did no harm to take him and it gave the anti-Grant papers material for editorial comment. The President's son was a second lieutenant in the Fourth Cavalry, three years out of West Point, but as aide-de-camp to Sheridan he held the brevet rank of lieutenant colonel at the age of twenty-four.

For guides Custer hired Charley Reynolds, a quiet man with a solid reputation; Louis Agard, a Frenchman who had served with Captain Raynolds in 1859; and Boston Custer, the frail young brother who had come out from the East to spend the summer. Frontiersmen would have snorted with derision had they learned that Boston, who knew nothing of the West and occasionally lost his way, was carried on the rolls as a guide. (Another Custer brother, Thomas, was commander of Company L with the brevet rank of lieutenant colonel.)

Newspaper correspondents began to send out dispatches. Samuel J. Barrows, of the New York *Tribune,* had been with the Yellowstone expedition in 1873 and knew the country. He was twenty-nine and a divinity student at Harvard, and in later years would become a Unitarian minister, editor of the *Christian Register,* and a Republican member of Congress from Massachusetts. Nathan H. Knappen, reporting for the Bismarck *Tribune,* was a tough-talking Westerner whose bias was unconcealed; he was in favor of finding the gold and not in favor of coddling the Indians. During the winter just past he had run his paper in the absence of the publisher, C. A. Lounsberry, and on one occasion had been fired on by an unhappy subscriber.

The star reporter, the true career journalist, was William Eleroy Curtis, reporting for the Chicago *Inter-Ocean* and the New York *World*. He was just twenty-three years old, a brand new member of the *Inter-Ocean* staff who was covering for the *World* on a free-lance basis. He would later serve Chicago newspapers for a quarter-century, and hold several government offices. His notions about Custer changed rapidly after his arrival at Fort Lincoln:

> He is a great man—a noble man is General Custer, and one of whom most of the world—that part which does not know him—has a singularly wrong idea. I came here expecting to find a big-whiskered, swearing, ranting, drinking trooper, and I found instead a slender, quiet gentleman, with a face as fair as a girl's, and manners as gentle and courtly as the traditional prince. Hunting for the drunken raider, I found a literary gentleman, in his library, surrounded by adjutants and orderlies, to whom he gave his military directions, while he wrote and read. . . . A few evenings since the writer, entering General Custer's library, saw a new phase of this man's character. He sat on a low stool by his desk, with a spelling-book in his hand; before him were two little girls, one white and the other colored, the children of his servants, whom he was affording the necessities denied by the lack of schools. . . . I have found that this has been his custom for several years, and all these little people of his household know of written words is what he has taught them.[16]

Under the command of Lieutenant George Wallace, the sixty-one spirited but well-disciplined Indian scouts were itching to get under way. Those who were Santees from the Nebraska agency had no quarrel with anyone, but the Arikaras whose families were at Fort Berthold were enraged

16. Chicago *Inter-Ocean*, July 19, 1874.

by the recent Sioux attack and wanted to see some action. Custer's chief Indian scout, Bloody Knife, held the rank of lance corporal and was thought of as a kind of personal aide to the General, although he was mustered with the other scouts. Lieutenant Wallace kept strict army records for these men, solemnly listing them on the descriptive rolls without exception as "eyes dark, complexion dark, hair black."

When the engineering detachment and the civilian scientists had arrived, Custer had a command of 951 soldiers and teamsters, and a sizable roster of military and civilian aides (see Appendix 4). He took them into camp for more training, sending the whole entourage to a location two miles below the fort on a tributary of the Heart. He wanted to toughen the men after long months of inactivity and he wanted to find out, while there still was time, what equipment they had forgotten and what they might advantageously leave behind.

The training was rough. No tents were taken; the men carried rations of hard bread, coffee, and meat in their haversacks; the allowance of one blanket per man was a stiff change from barracks life. To correspondent Curtis the experience was rather horrifying. Without much regard for accuracy in numbers, he wrote the *Inter-Ocean:*

> And just here for a moment let the reader imagine these 900 mules braying, 1,000 horses whinnying, the 300 cattle lowing, and the 2,000 men groaning through the dark and gloomy watches of the night because of these pestiferous mosquitoes, that make the valley of the Missouri the vilest place in the world. One lives with gloves and a head shield during the day, and sleeps in his shield and gloves, under blankets and bars during the night. Lift up your shield to speak to your neighbor, and in fifteen minutes after your lips and chin feel as mammoth as the Andes Mountains.

Take off your glove to button your collar closer, and your hand is a swollen and unseemly thing.[17]

In the final days Custer postponed his departure again to wait for a shipment of the newest cavalry weapons, the 1873 model .45 caliber Springfield carbine and the improved Colt's .45 pistol. He had been hounding the Rock Island arsenal for weeks to obtain these new issues because he felt inadequately armed with his old Sharp's .50 carbines and his .44 sidearms.

The whole country was now beginning to watch the project. Men were choosing sides according to conviction or interest: Westerners cheered and waited for news of a gold strike; Easterners tended to doubt the wisdom of the movement. Newspapers who hated Grant's administration blamed him personally for letting the Army tantalize the Indians. The Secretary of the Interior protested mildly and futilely to the Secretary of War. Bishop William H. Hare, a special commissioner to the Sioux, called the expedition "high-handed outrage" and warned of possible Indian retaliation.

Throughout the debate the Army stood firm on two points: (1) the chief purpose of the expedition was to conduct a much-needed reconnaissance, not to prospect for gold, and (2) it was *not* a violation of the 1868 treaty. The first argument was weakened by the fact that Custer was permitting two private miners to accompany him, but to have done less would have invited the wrath of the entire West. The Army's position on the treaty was best set forth by General Terry in a letter to General Sheridan: "I am unable to see that any just offense is given to the Indians by the expedition to the Black Hills. . . . From the earliest times the government has exercised the right of sending exploring parties of a military character into unceded territory, and this

17. Dispatch of June 30 in the issue of July 9, 1874.

expedition is nothing more." Terry cited the article of the treaty which permitted authorized officers and agents of the government to enter the reservation. As a member of the treaty commission, he could not believe that this provision was intended to exclude military forces, and he doubted if the Indians had so understood it.

"Can it be supposed," he asked, "that it was the intent of the treaty to set apart, in the heart of the national territory, a district nearly as great as the largest State east of the Mississippi River—two-thirds as large as the combined area of the six New England States—within which the government should be forbidden to exercise the power, which it everywhere else possesses, of sending its military forces where they may be required?"

At any rate, Terry concluded, the precedent had already been set. Since April 1869 three military posts had been established in the reservation for the protection of Indian agents, and two more were contemplated, and no one from the pro-Indian faction had complained.[18]

General Sherman took the same stand. Penning an endorsement on a copy of Terry's statement, he said, "I also was one of the commissioners to the Treaty of 1868, and agree with General Terry, that it was not intended to exclude the United States from exploring the Reservation for Roads, or for any other national purpose."[19]

The Indians thought otherwise and said so, devising a name for Custer's trail that expressed their bitterness. In negotiations for the Black Hills the following year, a chief named Fast Bear mentioned a road.

"What road?" one of the commissioners asked.

And Fast Bear replied grimly, "That thieves' road."

18. *Inter-Ocean,* July 27, 1874.
19. Sherman's sixth endorsement, Delano to Belknap, June 9, 1874, AGO, LR, 2275 (1874), NA.

The white-crowned wagons went out, four long lines reaching toward the west, on the morning of July 2. On either side the row of horsemen, with guidon pennants flying, reined in to keep their column from pulling ahead of the train. Up front, ahead of the ambulances and the artillery battery, sixteen musicians on white horses played "The Girl I Left Behind Me." Leading the formation was the buckskin-clad Custer on his prancing bay Dandy, and beside him rode young Fred Grant wearing a jaunty straw hat.

When they were out of sight of Fort Lincoln the bandsmen tossed their instruments into a wagon, the scouts broke up into details and took the lead, and parties of flankers strung themselves out to parallel the train far to the right and left. Custer's hounds dashed to and fro, flushing birds out of coulees and dodging clumps of prickly pear. For man and dog it was going to be a hot and tiring day, keeping up with the General.

CHAPTER 2

The Misery of Private Ewert

July 2 to July 14

The plan called for short marches on the first two days—
nothing strenuous until the men and animals were hardened
to the routine. "Yet there are men who will always remember those two days as the most cruel in the calendar of their
lives," wrote Samuel Barrows in his first dispatch from the
field. The heat was monstrous.

"They will never forget," Barrows said, "how, weak and
foot-sore, they fell down in the dusty trail under the merciless
sun and prayed for a cloud to shield them from its scorching
rays. They will not forget the death-like faintness that came
over them as they lay far in the rear of the vanishing train
and bade 'good-by' to the weary comrades who could afford
them no relief but some warm, sickening water from their
nearly empty canteens. . . . They will never forget, whatever be their habits, the priceless value of a clear, cold
draught of water."[1]

The men who fell ill were mainly infantrymen, and the
cause of their failure is not clear. They were accustomed to
longer marches than these. Company G of the Seventeenth
had made some marches of twenty-five and thirty miles coming up from the Grand River post, and both companies had
been in training for nearly two weeks since that time. Bar-

1. Barrows' dispatch of July 9 in the New York *Tribune*, Aug. 1,
1874.

rows attributed their illness to their drinking brackish water from pools and sloughs along the trail. Some of the sick men were put into the four ambulances, others rode the horses of the infantry officers, but some had to be left behind until camp was made and the ambulances could unload and return for them.

Men failed, but so did wagons. Recent rains had formed sloughs into which some of the vehicles sank to the hubs. Custer had gone ahead to find a campsite where wood and water were available, but when the train had been delayed for several hours in the mire, he decided to stop short of his goal and make a woodless camp. There were grass and water for the stock, but fuel for the cooking fires had to be carried two miles. Supper was late and scanty, and many of the teamsters—arriving after dark with tired and mud-spattered teams—went to sleep without a cup of coffee.

Still, the day was not ended for men who had set themselves the task of keeping a journal. For some, of course, it was mandatory. The scientists were expected to bring back a series of day-to-day observations. Custer had his official reports to write. Forsyth and Grant both were under instructions from Sheridan to keep daily logs. Professor A. B. Donaldson, of the scientific corps, had to prepare some articles for the St. Paul *Daily Pioneer* in addition to performing his regular tasks as botanist.

At least two of the enlisted men's journals have survived: those of Private William Zahn, of Company G, Seventeenth Infantry, and Private Theodore Ewert, Company H, Seventh Cavalry.

Zahn was barely literate and kept a perfunctory record. Of the first day's events he wrote, "Started out this morning in Rout for the Black Hills. Marched 14 miles and camped." Most of his daily entries for the next two months would be of a similar nature. "Pirty good water and pine trees," he would say when the country was friendly. When he had spent a hard day in the badlands he would simply write, "Poor water, no wood" without elaboration.[2]

Private Theodore Ewert was too talkative to be content with such laconic remarks. Often his facts were shaky and his opinions hastily formed, but he never hesitated to say what he thought at length. His journal provides some basic information not available in the reports of the officers and the reporters, and is our best source of detail about the attitudes and daily routine of the enlisted men.

Ewert's opinion of his commanding officer was frankly negative:

> Since the return of the "Yellowstone Expedition" on the 21st day of September 1873, General George A. Custer's restless spirit had been at work to devise a plausible excuse to enable him to visit the Black Hills district. . . . The unknown and unexplored Black Hills offered all inducements for more fresh laurels, and to enable him to gather these, no matter at what cost of labor, trouble, or life, became his study by night and by day. The honor of himself and his country weighed lightly in the scale against the "glorious?" name of "Geo. A. Custer," the hardships and danger to his men, as well as the probable loss of life were worthy of but little considerations when dim visions of an "Eagle" or even a "star" floated before the excited mind of our Lieut. Colonel. . . . The United States Government forgot its honor, forgot the sacred treaty in force between itself and the Dakota Sioux, forgot its integrity, and ordered the organization of an Expedition for the invasion of the Black Hills.[3]

2. Scrapbook of William Zahn, North Dakota Historical Society.
3. Journal of Private Theodore Ewert, July 2 to Aug. 30, 1874. Privately owned by Melma Huckeby Ewert, Jacksonville, Ill.

About the Indian policy of the government, Ewert was equally bitter:

> How is it that the many red murderers are not punished according to our laws? How is it that the Sioux chief "Red Cloud," the cause, author and instigator of the Fort Phil' Kearney massacre, is received at, and allowed to go about, certain frontier forts without being apprehended? Indian agents would lose their profitable situations, were every red scamp punished according to his deeds, and it is their living an easy life that makes them shield one of this brood from his punishment. Oh thou mighty and omnipotent, great and revered "Almighty Dollar'" thou makes mankind corrupt and rotten, for thy smile men commit murder, sacrifice every noble feeling, cut the throat of father, mother, brother or sister, to gain thee. . . . Why, in the name of justice and humanity, is not the Indian Bureow [sic] placed under control of the War Department?[4]

Only one other topic could draw such fervid prose from Private Ewert—the sad lot of the enlisted soldier:

> A soldier and his wife are liable to be parted at any minute and for any length of time, in the morning, at the noon-day meal, from the evening ramble, at the dead hour of night, whenever duty calls the soldier must obey and go, and the poor wife, sick or well, ill or dying, sees him go, with how heavy a heart God and herself alone knows, she cries as if her heart would break, for he goes on the trail of a marauding tribe of Indians, she is sure he will have to fight 'ere the return, and now, as he is hastily preparing, she is looking upon him, perhaps for the last time upon this earth.[5]

4. Ewert, p. 4.
5. Ibid., p. 6.

Despite his complaints, crotchety Private Ewert loved the army. He also admired Custer and could not always conceal it, though he always tried. Born in Prussia in 1847, Ewert came with his parents to Chicago at the age of 10, enlisted in the cavalry in 1861 at the age of 14. He served as a second lieutenant in the Twelfth Heavy Artillery for several months at the close of the Civil War, was mustered out in 1865, then enlisted as a private in the Thirty-Sixth Infantry in 1867. He was discharged as a corporal in 1869 and re-enlisted as a private in the Seventh Cavalry in 1871. His final discharge from the regular Army would come in 1883 when he would be discharged from the Fifth Infantry with the rank of sergeant major, but he would continue in the National Guard and attain the position of assistant adjutant general, Illinois National Guard, from 1902 to 1905.[6]

As trumpeter for Company H, and occasionally as orderly trumpeter for Custer, Private Ewert saw the expedition through the eyes of an enlisted man who had once been an officer. This kind of soldier usually views the privileges of the commissioned officer with utter sarcasm.

> The men raised no tents, as it was near midnight 'ere the horses were fed and groomed and the men got their supper, but the Officers, oh these gentlemen, they could not sleep these few hours without having their large wall-tents pitched, they did not have to put them up and the poor men, well what does an Officer care how tired or worn out, or even ill a man is, their imperial will would at all times, have to be obeyed, humanity is something that is foreign to their feelings and a little kindliness is but seldom or never shown to one of the rank and file.[7]

6. *Report of the Illinois Adjutant General, 1903–1904* (Springfield, Ill., 1904).
7. Ewert, p. 19.

TINTYPE OF A SOLDIER

Two days out, and clean-shaven youngsters now knew why so many of the older troopers wore full, drooping moustaches. The Dakota sun might strip the skin off a man's cheeks in patches and turn his nose into a scarlet, aching bulb, but if he had a moustache his upper lip, at least, was protected.

Crossing the alkali flats, the horses churned up billows of white alkaline powder that stuck to the sweating faces of the men and burned. At a shallow pond left by a recent storm, where the command stopped to rest, the air was filled with the braying of the tortured mules—thirsty, sore-backed, their fetlocks bloodied by prickly pear. At such a time a soldier could climb off his horse and sprawl on the ground, perhaps to watch Company A quarreling with Company B for the privilege of being first to fill canteens. In moments such as these, a man committed whole soul and forever to the indignities of army life at thirteen dollars a month— a man like Private Zahn—might have the wisdom to plop his black campaign hat over his eyes and catch five minutes of sleep. With a single line in his diary he could write off all the wretchedness of his day. "Long march, bad water, everboddy tired." But it was harder for a man like Ewert to accept his status.

Private Ewert's sky-blue trousers were reinforced at the seat with canvas for hard wear in the saddle, and his dark blue blouse of navy flannel grew heavier and darker as he sweated through a day's march. He wore short boots with yellow spurs. He hated his black, broad-rimmed felt hat because it was made of sleazy material. Had he been a corporal he could have worn, besides chevrons, a half-inch yellow strip down the outside of each trouser leg, and with promotion to sergeant he could have widened the strip to a full inch.

The heaviest parts of his uniform were in storage back home. These included his overcoat which, when rolled and tied, served as his pillow in the barracks; his dark blue uniform coat with yellow skirt facings; and a plumed black helmet for full dress, so heavy that it made his head ache. There also was a neat little blue forage cap, easier to wear than the brimmed campaign hat but affording less protection from the sun.[8]

In Custer's regiment the horses were assigned by color, with Company A riding coal-black mounts; C, G, and K riding sorrels; and so on. All trumpeters rode gray horses for easy identification, and Ewert's gray Monkey got a stiff workout on the days when Ewert was orderly trumpeter. After a long march, and while the column was still moving, the adjutant often gave Ewert a circular which had to be read and initialed by the commander of every company—including the rear guard—before camp could be made.

Monkey ate his grain ration from a nosebag and foraged for grass when staked out in the late afternoon. When brought in from grazing at retreat he was tied to a picket line along the company street until his master's trumpet sounded "boots and saddles" in the early dawn. If he threw a shoe the farrier gave him a new one, applying it so hot that it scorched the hoof. If he came down with the thumps, colic, or a sore back, he was doctored by regimental veterinary surgeon John M. Tempany. But generally his physical well-being and peace of mind were solely the responsibility of Private Ewert.

Considered alone, Monkey's saddle was a model of trimness and comfort—the traditional old McClellan saddletree

8. For the uniform of the enlisted soldier see AGO General Order 92, series 1872, printed copy in the library of the National Archives; and Circular No. 8, Office of the Surgeon-General, *A Report on the Hygiene of the United States Army* (Washington, 1875).

covered with black collar leather. But when the blanket, girth, flaps, sweat-leathers, and linen duck saddlebags were added, it began to grow cumbersome. When Ewert added his haversack, shelter tent, canteen, blankets, sidelines, lariat, and picket pin, then climbed into the saddle himself with a carbine, pistol, and sixty-four rounds of ammunition, Monkey was carrying about 220 pounds.

When the new carbines and pistols arrived at Fort Lincoln, just before the expedition began, the command had a single system of small arms for the first time. Until now, most of the men had carried Sharp's improved .50 caliber carbines, but there also had been many Ward Burton, Remington, and Springfield experimentals in the regiment. Custer had disliked having four patterns and four manuals, and had tried in 1873 to get his men equipped solely with Sharp's or Remington carbines. Terry had called his request "singular" and denied it, reminding him that the testing of experimental arms was a vital function.

The carbine that Private Ewert carried, and had fired very little, was the Army's best attempt since the Civil War to improve and unify its small-arms system. In 1873 a board of officers had recommended the adoption of the Springfield system for breechloading arms and the use of a .45 caliber bore for rifles, carbines, and pistols. In years to come there would be hot debate over the merits of the new rifle and carbine. They were single-shot weapons. Soldiers who carried them would often have to face Indians firing modern repeaters. Some cavalrymen felt that their carbines were hard to load while in motion, and that the breechblock was likely to be thrown open when the piece was dangling at the side of a trotting horse. There was to be much criticism of the breech mechanism, especially after Custer's disastrous battle in 1876.

About the new Colt's .45 pistol there was much more

agreement. Other revolvers might be easier to load, have a bit more striking power, and wear longer, but the Colt's had one overwhelming advantage—it shot straightest. It was a welcome replacement for the varied assortment of .44 pistols the regiment had been using, including 200 Colt's, 223 Remingtons, and 36 Smith & Wesson revolvers, and 147 old Remington .50 caliber single-barrel breech-loaders.

The four artillery pieces which lumbered along at the head of the wagon train, drawn by condemned cavalry mounts, included three Gatling guns and a three-inch Rodman. The Gatlings were a new development in ordnance, and the men were impressed by the rapidity with which the revolving barrels could fire .45 caliber cartridges. Good insurance, the Gatlings, and the Rodman fieldpiece would be useful for shelling patches of woods or dispersing masses of Indians.[9]

A man's diet on the march was mostly bread and meat. Seldom was there time to cook beans, and certainly not time enough to boil soup for the five hours specified in paragraph 117 of *Army Regulations*.

Bread could mean brittle wafers of almost imperishable hardtack, officially termed "hard bread," that came from the supply depot packed in boxes. Once a few cakes of it had been removed, the remaining pieces jiggled themselves to bits inside the box. Bread could also mean hot, soft bread made by the company cooks when there was time. Custer carried hard bread and flour in a ratio of three to one.

Of meat there was a good variety, ranging from the bacon that a man could carry in his haversack for a noon lunch,

9. Discussion of soldiers' arms is based on a letter from Alfred Terry to Acting Adjutant General, Division of Missouri, April 9, 1874, enclosing a report of arms in use in the Department of Dakota, No. 1573 (1874), RG 98, NA.

to the tender slabs of venison killed on the march and cooked for supper. The beef herd was there to fall back on, but so plentiful were the pronghorn antelope, mule deer, and white-tailed deer, that many of the beeves would still be ambling along at the end of the expedition, fatter than the day they started.

Rio coffee, boiled black and bitter, supplemented the ration, along with rice, sugar, vinegar, salt, pepper, and tobacco. For delicacies beyond these a man must turn to the sutler's wagons. Officially the sutler had been called "post trader" since 1868, but the older term persisted. A few days before the expedition started, Custer forbade the sale of liquor to enlisted men and teamsters because he wanted everyone sober for the departure.[10] Now the ban was off and the men could buy whiskey at John W. Smith's wagons with the usual restriction: they must drink it at the counter.

When he was orderly trumpeter for the regiment, Private Ewert's day began at 2:30 A.M. He stepped blinking from the guard tent with his bugle, sounded "first call for reveille," to alert the camp. Company cooks began to rattle the mess gear, and the teamsters shuffled to the picket line to harness their cranky mules in the dark. At 2:45, when Ewert sounded "reveille," the day officially began. Half an hour later came "breakfast call." Coffee, hard bread, and bacon. The "general," a call ordering tents to be struck and all wagons packed, came at 4:15. There was no appeal from this call, so the officer who lagged to finish a letter to his wife or eat a bit more breakfast might find his tent flattened about his head as the camp guard yanked the pegs. Cooking equipment went into the mess chests, the mess chests were slid into the company wagons, and the cooks kicked out the fires.

10. General Order No. 50, June 27, 1874, Fort Abraham Lincoln.

Ewert sounded "boots and saddles," the signal to saddle up, and then "stand to horse." When the men had counted off by fours, the company commanders sang out "prepare to mount" and "mount," and the expedition was ready for the "advance." By 5 A.M. the wheels were turning; dust in the nostrils before sunrise.

In the afternoon, when Custer had chosen a campsite, his battalion commanders immediately threw out a strong line of mounted and dismounted pickets. Before the first wagon had drawn up to its station, these pickets or vedettes had occupied a commanding line of several hundred yards about the camp. Outside this line the scouts posted pickets of their own. The rest of the men set about making camp.

As shown in the photograph (Figure 2), camp was laid out as a hollow square. In the distance is the line of infantry tents, with the parked wagons in the foreground and the two cavalry battalions forming the sides. Regimental head-quarters tents are inside the square beyond the wagons, and the cooks' tents are behind their companies outside the square. At retreat the mules are brought in and tied to the wagons and the cavalry mounts are tethered to a line in front of the men's tents.

Camp-making could be an orderly process if done in fair weather and daylight, with the prospect of a leisurely evening ahead. It could be a nightmare, though, in darkness and rain, if the unhappy troopers had been delayed by a poor trail. By the time the men had tended their horses, waited on the officers, eaten a rained-on supper, and rolled them-selves into their blankets, it might be past midnight. Private Ewert could be expected to have an opinion on the subject:

> You may ask "Did not the Officers stand exposed to these storms and rains as well as the rank and file?" I answer emphatically, No! As soon as a storm was seen

approaching, four, six or eight men were called upon to stretch the Captains or Lieutenants tent, and as soon as the first pins were driven these would step inside dry and comfortable, while poor Pat, Hans or Dick could stand in the storm and finish driving the pins, and then, already wet through and through, he could go and pitch his own little dog-tent, under which he would be shelter'd hardly better than under the sky. And even if an Officer did get wet he could go into his tent and change for dry under-clothing, but a poor unfortunate "buck-private," unable to boast of such a thing, as a dry change, would have to let the heat of his body evaporate the rain.[11]

LOGGING THE MILES

Custer delayed his departure from the first day's camp, on the headwaters of the Little Heart, to give the mules a chance to graze. Before the "advance" sounded he finished a letter to Mrs. Custer and sent it back to Fort Lincoln with a scout. All was well, he said, and his new colored cook named Johnson had fixed him hot biscuits last night, despite the late hour. He was sending Mrs. Custer a young curlew that he had picked up on the prairie.[12]

When the column began to move at 7:45 A.M., someone in the flurry of packing forgot to load the three boards which Custer was using as a bed. His wife, Elizabeth, recalled the incident later in Boots and Saddles: "During the entire sum-

11. For daily routine, see Barrows' dispatch of July 9 in the New York Tribune, Aug. 1, 1874; General Order No. 1, Black Hills Expedition; George A. Forsyth, The Story of a Soldier (New York, 1900), pp. 160–67; and Ewert, p. 21.

12. Elizabeth B. Custer, Boots and Saddles (New York, 1885), pp. 298–99.

mer, owing to this piece of forgetfulness, the mattress was laid down every night on ground that was always uneven and sometimes wet."[13]

Private Ewert would have been delighted to know that. With the thermometer at 101, the course led through a sterile stretch of rocky hills, shrubless and poorly watered, and grasshoppers rose up before the column in fluttering hordes. The campsite was a plateau on the headwaters of Chanta Peta Creek. "A small stream, a mere wet-weather brook, rises here and furnishes us with stagnant water," wrote Professor Donaldson. Distance covered, 14.1 miles, and again some of the infantrymen fainted. (See Appendix 1 for a complete table of camps and distances.)

Back at Fort Lincoln on the morning of July 5 a party of Sioux ran off a herd of cattle and some horses they found along the Heart. The infantrymen left to defend the post had no means of chasing the thieves, and could only watch the livestock hustled away in a cloud of dust. Reporting the loss to General Terry, Captain John S. Poland said he thought the thirty or forty Indians were from Two Bears' band at the Grand River Agency, and he added the hope that the Indian ponies might become infected with glanders, a disease with which two of the stolen horses were suffering.[14] There was no excitement to match this in Custer's command, but the first accident occurred when a teamster was thrown from a mule and was run over by his wagon at a bad crossing. A horse was struck on the leg by a rattlesnake, and the veterinarian saved the animal by making an incision and applying a tourniquet. (The journals of the expedition contain few references to rattlesnakes, although Luther North, in a letter to his uncle, said the ground was alive

13. Ibid., p. 302n.
14. Poland to Acting Adjutant General, Department of Dakota, July 5, 1874, Fort Abraham Lincoln, LS, RG 98, NA.

with them. It was common practice for soldiers in the West to beat the ground for snakes before pitching tents.) After a march of 16.9 miles the expedition camped by a stream which the Indians called "The Creek Where the Bear Winters."

Pronghorn antelope country lay ahead. The jagged horizon had smoothed to a swell of rolling plain that was well grassed and watered. On the morning of July 6 the photographer Illingworth, riding alone and out of sight of the train, estimated that he saw 300 pronghorns at once. Nothing excited Custer so much as wild game—excited him even to acts of poor judgment. Once on the Kansas prairie he had left his command while chasing buffalo, had accidentally shot his horse, and risked being cut off by Indians. He was under orders from Mrs. Custer to stay closer to his column on this trip, but he wandered often with his Remington sporting rifle, his fast horse, and his band of eager hounds.

When Illingworth came back with a pair of pronghorns, the entire regiment caught the fever to go hunting. Several parties went out and the firing grew more and more promiscuous. Ahead of the column, Custer had just drawn a bead on a fine buck when it was shot by some of the scouts. Disgusted, the General fired two shots over their heads so close that they left their saddles and flattened themselves on the ground.

There was a standing order against firing within the column, but when the white rumps of the scampering pronghorns began to flash before the eyes of the soldiers, no one could resist. Professor Donaldson told it this way:

> A herd of seven antelope, led by a fine buck ran across the advancing columns and within ten or fifteen feet of the battery of artillery. The temptation was too great for mortals to resist, and whole volleys were

discharged contrary to orders. The cannoniers did not
have time to unlimber their ordnance, but blazed
away with their revolvers. The noble buck fell com-
pletely riddled through, while, marvelous to relate,
the balance of the herd escaped. The driver of one of
the four-horse teams drawing a Gatlin gun, left his
post for a moment to salute the herd with his six-
shooter. His team became frightened and ran away, and
for a few minutes a Gatlin gun made a series of rapid
evolutions over the plains of Dakota, in a manner
wholly unrecognized in military practice.[15]

Both wheel horses were thrown down, Private Ewert
said, upsetting the gun but injuring nobody. The driver was
made to march on foot with the infantry for the rest of the
day. It was a form of punishment the infantrymen may
have considered mild, but walking in cavalry boots was not
quite the same as walking in infantry shoes.

That night the regiment camped on the north fork of
the Cannonball. It was the best water they had seen thus far,
a stream up to seventy-five feet wide, flowing swiftly over
a shaly bed through a wooded valley. The men bathed,
washed a few articles of clothing, and tried to catch some
fish. No luck fishing, but there was plenty of pronghorn
steak for supper. Distance logged, 12.9 miles.

As if to make up for the time he had squandered hunting,
Custer pushed his men hard the next day, July 7, and
marched 30.4 miles. The real reason for the long haul was
topographic; Custer was aiming for running water in the
south fork of the Cannonball. It was a smaller stream than
the north fork, milk-white water perhaps twenty feet across,
and went down in the official record as Cedar Creek. Be-

15. Donaldson's dispatch of July 7 in St. Paul *Daily Pioneer*, July 28,
1874.

tween it and the stream they had left the night before, the men found nothing but alkali pools, unpleasant for drinking.

"By someone's blunder," wrote Donaldson, "the whole train was misled about one mile and had to turn about. . . . All came into camp weary and worn, hungry, thirsty and faint. Before the train was over, and the men ready for a short rest, it was nearly midnight."

Imperturbable William Zahn set down another entry in his sketchy record: "Marched 31 miles and made a Poor camp Hardly no wood and water."

Ewert described the location as the junction of Cedar Creek and the Prettystone River, "and tho' I tried hard, I could find neither cedar nor pretty stones, therefore fell asleep wondering, by what stretch of imagination a man could be justified in naming these streams as above." He would have the answer tomorrow, as far as the Prettystone was concerned, when he marched over the Belle Pierre Hills —so called because of the colored pebbles that abounded there.

After so hard a march, the command was hoping for a late reveille. Instead, at 3 A.M. an alarm turned every man out under arms. The picket at vedette post No. 3 had opened fire, after a challenge, at what he thought was a band of Indians creeping through the grass. His imagination had tricked him. By the time the corporal of the guard had investigated and discovered the error, the entire regiment was standing in rank and ready for deployment. "The men are always mad," Ewert said, "when told that no Indians are around, waiting to attack the camp and that they can return to their blankets."[16]

One man missed all the excitement. A private from Com-

16. Ewert, pp. 10–12.

pany B appeared just as camp was being broken the next
morning, to explain why he had been absent without leave
since the night of July 6. He had become intoxicated that
night, had fallen asleep at the edge of camp, and when he
awoke he found that the regiment had moved out. (His
company commander, First Lieutenant Benjamin Hodgson,
had noted his absence and taken his horse along.) The soldier
had hidden himself all day on July 7 and set out on the
trail after dark. He made the thirty-one miles during the
night and arrived in time for roll call July 8.

The campsite this day was on the north side of Bois Caché
or Hiddenwood Creek, a tributary of the Grand River. "A
cluster of trees about as big as a New England garden," said
reporter Curtis in the *Inter-Ocean*. Curtis marveled at the
ability of the scout named Goose to lead the command nine-
teen miles across those barren hills and find a spot so well
concealed that it could not be seen from a distance of two
miles.

When the train moved out July 9 it had come 123 miles
from Fort Lincoln. No real trouble, no illness except the
temporary indisposition of the infantrymen. Today's trail
sloped down into the valley of the north fork of the Grand,
a foot-deep ribbon of sweet but muddy water in a mile-wide
valley. During the day the column crossed a pony trail two
days old, leading from the Powder River country toward
the agencies on the Missouri. To liven the day, old Goose
told the men that the trail had been made by hostiles who
were taking meat and hides down to the reservations and
would then come back, on fresh ponies, to attack the column
in the Black Hills. But Private Ewert, tired from seven days
in the saddle, was not very impressed. His journal entry was
reminiscent of Private Zahn's one-line summaries of all that
was unpleasant about cavalry expeditions. "Grass was scarce
and poor and no wood."

By now the teamsters had herded their mules across some miserable alkali flats and had made a few bad crossings, but the worst country for wagons still lay ahead. The July 10 route led up the valley of the north fork of the Grand. Fred Grant's journal says the column crossed Lightning Creek and Buffalo Creek, then made two crossings of the Grand. Colonel Ludlow's chart shows only three crossings. The campsite was on the north side of the Grand, a muddy stream with considerable current, and the column again crossed to the south side soon after breaking camp on the following morning.

July 11 brought the expedition to the Cave Hills after twenty miles of uphill marching over a sterile land armored with cactus. On the eastern side of a ridge several miles long, where the first pine timber was seen, Custer visited a cave which he christened Ludlow's Cave. The wagon train slogged on into a camp not far away.

Next day, July 12, was the worst the expedition had experienced. Along the tributaries of the Grand, tortuous gullies creased the route. Of the eleven miles traveled, four were spent in futile searching for wagon crossings. At times like these, Custer's reputation as a trailblazer was at stake, and even Private Ewert trusted his ability to take the train through. (Ewert said that Custer was "not used to being thwarted, even by nature.")

The pioneer company was well equipped with shovels, picks, and axes to clear a route for the train. When a gulch was found that wagons could not cross unaided, a grade was made by shaving down the steep sides. If the obstacle was a stream, a bridge was quickly built. Custer always picked the location of the bridge himself, grabbed a shovel, and directed the work while shoveling. Usually a solid crossing could be made with stones, sod, or willow branches. If not, the wagonmaster shouted "poles!" The teamsters climbed out of the saddles and brought up the spare coupling poles that every wagon carried, and laid them across the stream in two or three layers. Then the crevices were filled with brush, sod, or rushes mowed with scythes, and the structure was finished.

To test his bridge the General sent the ambulances across first, then the artillery. If the wheels of the lighter carriages cut through, the bridge was strengthened before the big wagons rumbled down to the crossing.

William Eleroy Curtis, in the *Inter-Ocean,* paid a tribute to the ordeal of the off-wheel mules during a bridge crossing. Half a dozen teamsters were always standing at the bridge to help whip the mules across, and their blows usually fell on the off-wheeler.

> If I was an "off-wheeler" I should memorialize Congress to have the position of assistant mule-whacker abolished. You see these men—these assistants—stand in the middle of the gulch, and the wagons go down so quickly that the leading mules run under while their whips are in the air; but the "off-wheeler" gets along just in time to catch the downward stroke, and as the tug comes in going up the other side, the assistants generally get time to whack him again before he is out of trouble. While the wagons are waiting at one of these gulches . . . you hear an occasional bray, about one-sixth as many brays as there are mules on the wagons. It is the off-wheeler. It is simply a short, subdued bray, but it means a great deal.[17]

17. Curtis' dispatch of July 14 in the *Inter-Ocean,* July 30, 1874. See also S. J. Barrows, "The Northwestern Mule and His Driver," *Atlantic Monthly,* 35 (May 1875), 556. For drawings showing contract specifications for army wagons in use during and after the Civil War, see *Specifications for Means of Transportation . . . for Use in the United States Army* (Washington, GPO, 1882).

The column marched and countermarched, probing among the clay knobs and gullies, and finally camped seven airline miles from their point of departure in the morning. During the next day, July 13, they moved across cactus-laden alkali flats and spanned dry channels, finding no water except in stagnant ponds. There were scattered buttes, flat-topped or pinnacled, loaf-shaped or domed, all girdled by belts of stratified clay in white, black, blue, brown, and red. While Captain Thomas McDougall and scout Charley Reynolds were hunting away from the column, an Indian started from a ravine about two thousand yards away and rode hurriedly off. Another followed him, and the hunters soon had counted twenty braves leaving the scene.[18]

Said Private Ewert, "Our horses were in constant misery, their fetlocks were pierced by thousands of cactus needles, causing our trail to be spotted with quite an amount of blood."

But a great day was dawning tomorrow. They were near a valley of cool water and high grass in an area called the Short Pine Hills, near the Montana border. Everyone but the scouts was surprised to find this treasure, and every journal bore a happy entry. The wagons pulled up into orderly ranks, the mules flapped their great ears at the sight of endless grass, and the word ran through the command that at last there was enough water to wash one's underwear. Because the outlook was cheery now, and the Black Hills were but sixty miles away, Custer named the location Prospect Valley.

18. George A. Custer to Elizabeth Custer, July 15, 1874, in Marguerite Merington, ed., *The Custer Story: The Life and Intimate Letters of General George A. Custer and His Wife Elizabeth* (New York, 1950), p. 273.

CHAPTER 3

The Scientific Corps

July 15 to July 22

Custer was sending two scouts back to Fort Lincoln with a
letter to Elizabeth and a packet of official mail, and everyone in camp was scrawling notes to go into the saddlebags.
The allowance for each company was but a few ounces, and
how this tiny ration was apportioned is not clear. Even
Private Ewert, in a preferred position as orderly trumpeter
for the day, was glad when Custer's private secretary,
Thomas Crosby, let him send out two very thin letters.

To no one's surprise, officers were given a larger share of
the precious allowance. In the *Inter-Ocean,* William Eleroy
Curtis presented this description of a young officer writing
to his admirers back home:

> Fancy, oh, bespangled butterfly, your brass-buttoned,
> gold-laced chevalier in a faded flannel shirt, and
> trowsers seated with canvas! Fancy him seated on the
> grass under the sutler's tent, leaning against a whisky
> barrel, and picking his teeth with a straw. Unshaven
> . . . the mustache you thought "so military" lost in the
> scraggly growth of sun-bleached beard; those eyes that
> looked with such passionate fervor into yours, blood-
> shot and swollen by the heat and wind; those lips
> which—which whispered so fondly those sweet noth-
> ings, blistered and broken into great black patches; his

faultless cravat exchanged for a red bandanna; that *distingue* foot covered with an army brogan and a pair of clanking spurs. This is your hero now, but he doesn't forget what he once was, and gets his letters ready for the mail.[1]

Two Arikara scouts, Skunk's Head and Bull Neck, left camp after dark on the night of July 15, planning to ride by night and rest by day. They were well mounted and armed, carrying rations for four days, and were happy to be returning to their wives and children on the Missouri. A part of their burden of mail was for public consumption: the reportage of the newspaper correspondents. Another part was for the information of General Terry in St. Paul, General Sheridan in Chicago, and General Sherman in Washington; but it, too, was written with an eye to public reaction. Custer's official dispatch to Terry was given to the press and widely reprinted as soon as it reached St. Paul.

This expedition reached this point yesterday having marched since leaving Fort Lincoln two hundred and twenty seven and a half miles. We are now one hundred and seventy miles in a direct line from Lincoln and within five miles of the Little Missouri river and within about twelve miles of the Montana boundary. . . . The health of my command is something remarkable, not a single man being on the sick report. Every one seems not only in good health, but in excellent spirits. . . . Our march thus far has been made without molestation upon the part of the Indians. We discovered no signs indicating the recent presence of Indians until day before yesterday when Captain McDougall 7th Cavalry who was on the flank discovered

1. Curtis' dispatch of Aug. 3 in the *Inter-Ocean* of Aug. 27, 1874.

a small party of about twenty Indians watching our
movements, the Indians scampered off as soon as discovered. Yesterday the same or a similar sized party
made its appearance along our line of march and soon
after several signals of smoke were sent up which our
Indian guides interpret as carrying information to the
main body of our presence and movements. As I sent
pacific messages to all the tribes infesting this region
before the expedition moved and expressed a desire to
maintain friendly relations with them, the signals observed by us may have simply been made to enable
the villages to avoid us. Our Indian guides think differ-
ently however and believe the Indians mean war,
should this be true they will be the party to fire the first
shot. Indians have been seen near camp to-day. Mr.
Grinnell of Yale College one of the Geologists accompanying the expedition discovered on yesterday an
important fossil, it was a bone about four feet long
and twelve inches in diameter and had evidently belonged to an animal larger than an elephant. Beds of
lignite of good quality have been observed at various
points along our route by Professor Winchell one of
the Geologists of the expedition. I do not know whether
I will be able to communicate with you again before
the return of the expedition or not.[2]

Custer's reference to geological findings was a sign of his
times. A chunk of fossil bone, a vein of dark lignite sand-
wiched in the earth, a new grassy valley, these were things
of public interest in the days of westward migration. It was

2. Custer to the Acting Adjutant General, Department of Dakota
[July 15, 1874], in a fragment of Custer's order and dispatch book,
Western Americana Collection, Yale University Library. Reprinted with
slight variations by Oharra.

not just commonsense interest—people needing to know
what lay ahead of them—but was a characteristic of men's
minds when an entire nation lived closer to the phenomena
of nature. Most army officers had a smattering of knowledge
about natural history. Physicians were versed in botany.
Hunters, ranchers, miners knew the elements of the wilder-
ness by name. A man could call his sagebrush Artemisia if
he liked, and talk about the quartzite and feldspar in the
ridge behind his barn, and nobody thought it queer or
uncommon.

In a land so vast the data accumulated slowly. Each time
a column of soldiers probed another unexplored region, taking along a geologist or botanist from an Eastern university
and a unit from the Corps of Engineers, something new was
added to man's scrapbook of facts. The tortuous ribbons of
charted country that resulted from these expeditions eventually crisscrossed themselves into a network of ever-
broadening bands.

Working under Army or Department of Interior supervision, a handful of scientists and topographers had undertaken the gigantic assignment of charting the West. Great
surveys of the 1850s, during the search for railroad routes,
had resulted in a magnificent multi-volume work called
*Reports of Explorations and Surveys to Ascertain the Most
Practicable and Economic Route for a Railroad from the
Mississippi River to the Pacific Ocean.* These offered a wealth
of findings on flora and fauna, geography and geology.

Even now as Custer's command rested in Prospect Valley,
exploration was going on throughout the West. Lieutenant
George M. Wheeler was in charge of a program of surveys
and explorations west of the 100th meridian, involving
areas of California, Nevada, Nebraska, Utah, Arizona,
Colorado, New Mexico, Wyoming, and Montana. Geologist
Clarence King was surveying the 40th parallel from the

eastern slope of the Rockies to the Sierra Nevada. Dr. Ferdinand V. Hayden, who had fired the West with his belief in
Black Hills gold, was exploring down in Colorado. Major
J. W. Powell was working in Wyoming, Utah, and Arizona.
(The U.S. Geological Survey, which eventually would cen-
tralize the work of all such scientists, would not be established for another five years.[3])

When General Sheridan had ordered Custer into the field
he had not planned to send a scientific corps. The trip was
to be a rapid reconnaissance, the kind that scientists hated
because it gave them little time to investigate the land. He
had, however, extended an invitation to Professor Othniel C.
Marsh, famous Yale paleontologist, who was his personal
friend. Marsh was an enthusiastic collector and classifier of
fossil remains in the West, and one of America's earliest
boosters of the Darwinian theory of natural selection.
Sheridan had written Marsh in May: "I do not intend to let
Gen'l Custer be embarrassed by any outside people except
yourself if you should desire to go, and extend to you an
invitation. . . . I do not know when you will have such an
opportunity."[4]

Marsh declined but sent his young assistant, George Bird
Grinnell. For a while Grinnell was the only scientist sched-
uled to go; but out in the Department of Dakota there was
much sentiment favoring the addition of a geologist. Colonel
Ludlow, already assigned to the command as engineering
officer, wired his superiors in Washington for permission
to hire a geologist at $150 a month. He was told that the

        3. Engineer Department, U.S. Army, *Report upon the United States
Geographical Surveys West of the One Hundredth Meridian. Vol. I:
Geographical Report* (Washington, GPO, 1889). Appendix F, pp. 418–
745, is a summary of explorations and surveys between the Mississippi
River and the West Coast from 1500 to 1880.
        4. Charles Suchert and Clara Mae LeVene, *O. C. Marsh, Pioneer in
Paleontology* (New Haven, 1940), p. 142n.

Chief of Engineers had no objection in principle but had no money in his current budget to pay the salary.[5]

In the meantime General Custer, at Fort Lincoln, was thinking of a geologist also. He wired Terry on May 30: "Is there no way by which the service of a geologist can be had with the expedition? The country to be visited is so new and believed to be so interesting that it will be a pity not to improve to the fullest extent the opportunity to determine all that is possible of its character, scientific and otherwise."[6]

All this circumlocution might have been boiled down to a simple question: May I look for gold?

Finally the Army got its scientific corps without the prospect of taxing its engineering budget. The state of Minnesota provided the geologist, Newton H. Winchell, and seems to have paid the way of the botanist, A. B. Donaldson. Grinnell and his assistant, Luther North, were coming along with the understanding that they were to create no expense to the government; apparently they were financed by Marsh at Yale.

After the start of the new fiscal year, when the Chief of Engineers received his annual allocation, Colonel Ludlow was able to obtain money to pay Professor Winchell $450.[7] The Army, then, did not get its scientific data free, but the intent of the War Department was plain: no extensive body of experts was desired, the expedition was not thought of as a scientific one, and certainly the discovery of gold was not uppermost in the minds of Belknap, Sherman, and Sheridan.

5. Ludlow to Chief of Engineers, May 23, 1874, and Chief of Engineers to Ludlow, June 1, 1874, LR, Chief of Engineers, No. 1002 (1874), RG 77, NA.

6. Custer to Terry, May 30, 1874, LR, Division of the Missouri, No. 997 (1874), RG 98, NA.

7. A note on Grinnell's agreement to provide his own expenses is in the 1874 box, Sheridan Papers, Library of Congress.

With the addition of photographer William H. Illingworth, the civilian corps was complete. Illingworth, as a
man with an important job who did mysterious things with
glass plates and bottles of chemicals, was also considered by
the military to be a man of science. For the enlisted men, one
term sufficed to classify the geologist, zoologist, botanist,
and photographer. They were "bug hunters."

GEORGE BIRD GRINNELL AND LUTHER NORTH

Grinnell was a senior at Yale in 1870 when Marsh had
organized the first student expedition to the fossil beds of
Nebraska, Kansas, and Colorado. As one of twelve students
on that tour, he had become fascinated by the country and
had returned two years later to hunt buffalo; but his love
for paleontology had soon called him back to Marsh's labora-
tory. In 1873 he had been named assistant in paleontology
at the Peabody Museum of Natural History at Yale. He was
twenty-four years old when Marsh sent him out to join the
Black Hills group.

In later years Grinnell would serve a long period as
editor of *Forest and Stream,* would be instrumental in the
preservation of Yellowstone and Glacier National Parks,
would organize the first Audubon Society, and become a
well-known student of North American ethnology.[8] With
Custer he was playing a dual role as zoologist and paleontologist and, although he knew how to take care of himself, he
was glad to have Luther North at hand.

North was hardly trained to be an assistant zoologist;
his real task was to guide Grinnell through the buttes and
coulees and help him collect specimens. The two men had
met in 1872 when North had served as Grinnell's guide on

8. Biographical data on Grinnell are from Suchert and *Who's Who
in America,* 1899–1900.

a buffalo hunt. Guiding young Easterners was North's civilian vocation, but he had made a name for himself shortly after the Civil War as one of the leaders of the famed Pawnee Battalion. He and his brother Frank had worked at the Pawnee Agency in Nebraska in 1860–63 and knew those Indians well. Frank had been asked to raise a company of a hundred scouts to fight the Sioux and Cheyennes along the Nebraska frontier in 1864, and because the outfit had done well, a battalion of two hundred warriors had been formed in 1867 to patrol the Union Pacific Railroad then inching toward the Rockies. Luther, who had been an enlisted soldier in the Second Nebraska Cavalry during the war, then accepted a captaincy in the Pawnee Battalion as commander of Company D.[9]

Grinnell collected some specimens and he compiled lists of mammals and birds, some of which he only observed or heard about.[10] He neither collected nor mentioned arthropods, amphibians, reptiles, or fishes, and his lists of mammals and birds often give evidence of the haste with which they had to be assembled. Moving hurriedly across the plains, Grinnell had little time to bother with small mammals such as rats, mice, or shrews, and he saw only one specimen of a common small rodent of the region, Richardson's ground squirrel. Of the larger mammals, however, he made a fair collection.

9. Some years later, Grinnell would record the exploits of the Norths in a book called *Two Great Scouts and Their Pawnee Battalion* (New York, 1928). See also Addison E. Sheldon, "The North Brothers and the Pawnee Nation," *Nebraska History, 15* (1934), 297–304.

10. All references to the official reports of the scientific team are from William Ludlow, *Report of a Reconnaissance of the Black Hills of Dakota* (Washington, GPO, 1875). Ludlow's preliminary report also appears in the *Annual Report* of the Chief of Engineers, 1874, and in various newspapers—including the New York *Tribune,* Sept. 14, and the *Army and Navy Journal,* Sept. 19, 1874.

On the open plains, the most obvious animal was the pronghorn antelope. Grinnell watched and recorded the efforts of the soldiers to kill this fast and rugged creature. "In proportion to its size, it is more tenacious of life than the grizzly bear," he wrote, "and from its astonishing speed it is often enabled to escape even after having received a wound that would have brought a deer or an elk immediately to the ground." He saw one pronghorn outrun Charley Reynolds' horse for more than two miles after Reynolds' rifle had broken one foreleg at the knee and one hind leg just below the knee.

Two other mammals of the plains could move with great speed. Grinnell watched a jackrabbit, scooting over the short grass with frenzied leaps, outdistance Custer's leggy wolf-hounds for two miles before it was caught. The kit fox, a handsome little buff-yellow fox with big ears and a black-tipped tail, was good for half a mile against the voracious hounds.

Black-tailed prairie dogs were everywhere, squatting like scale-model woodchucks on the mounds that rimmed their burrows. The thirteen-lined ground squirrel abounded on the plains but was not seen in the piney hills. All the flowing streams contained the muskrat and the larger ones supported beaver.

Though none was seen, Grinnell thought there still might be bison in the Black Hills region. In Prospect Valley he found the skull of an old bull with part of the hide still attached, and later he discovered the lower jaw of a cow with the periosteum still on it. Otherwise, the only evidence of the once numerous bison were the chalk-white bones that dotted the prairie. In one place the Indians had arranged a collection of skulls ceremonially, painting them red and blue and placing them in five parallel rows of twelve each, all facing east.

The coyote occurred in great numbers on the high table-lands near the Hills, and were numerous on the plains, but Grinnell would see none after entering the Hills. In the higher elevations they would be replaced by the gray wolf, seen singly or by twos and threes, "sneaking along the mountain sides or crossing the narrow valleys."

Within the Hills, Grinnell would collect, observe, or find evidence of the mule deer, elk, bighorn, mountain lion, and grizzly bear.

Before leaving Fort Lincoln, Grinnell could have named with reasonable accuracy the birds he would find on the expedition. The region drained by the Missouri and its tributaries had been well studied, and the Black Hills were unlikely to yield any surprises. The most recent example of the considerable amount of ornithological literature on the region was the 791-page *Birds of the Northwest* by Elliott Coues, published in 1874 by the Department of Interior. Apparently Grinnell had not yet seen a copy when he compiled his own list in the same year; it may not have come off the presses of the Government Printing Office until later in the year. His own final list contained 110 species of birds.

The task of fossil-hunting which Grinnell shared with Winchell proved disappointing. Two days out of Fort Lincoln, a few freshwater shells were discovered, then a whole week passed without the discovery of a single fossil. The column simply moved too rapidly for thorough searching. The worst country for traveling was the best for fossil-hunting, and in the badlands—where Grinnell and Winchell might have found something if allowed more time—it was necessary to press on toward water and grass.

"Four scientific gentlemen have been wandering about with bags and hammers for nearly a week," wrote Curtis, "and not yet have they found one [fossil] of importance. It seems that nothing ever died in this region, and one is inclined to the opinion that nothing ever existed here until foolish, restless man penetrated these barren plains."[11]

The large vertebrate remains mentioned by Custer in his report were found at Castle Butte, about six miles north of Prospect Valley. Grinnell described them as "the crushed and flattened leg bone of some enormous animal and a few fragmentary turtle bones, all so fragile and weathered that we were unable to transport them to camp." At first he thought the big leg bone was from a mastodon, but further study indicated that it probably was the femur of a dinosaur. Several days later a few fragments of rib came to light from what was probably the giant *Brontotherium,* but in the main the entire lot of fossils discovered on the expedition were marine specimens—shells from the ancient seas—including two new species.

NEWTON H. WINCHELL

Geologically speaking, there were strong family ties between the Black Hills, which now lay immediately to the south of Custer's camp, and the Rockies farther to the west. The fierce upboiling of liquid rock, the eons of calm sedimentation, the shifting, buckling, tilting movements of the earth's skin that made the Rockies—these forces made the Black Hills at the same time. At the center of the Hills was a crystalline core of granitic rock, squeezed from the interior of the planet. Circling this inner formation was a plateau of limestone, deeply sliced by canyons. Around the plateau was a broad and open valley, its floor brick red from the sands and shales that later would be known to geologists as the Spearfish Red Beds. Overlooking the valley and surrounding the inner hills like a wall was an outer ring of

11. Curtis' dispatch of July 11 in the *Inter-Ocean* of July 30, 1874.

sandstone "hogbacks," upturned ages ago and worn bare of the clays that once had covered them. The few gaps that watercourses had cut through this wall were the only passages into the Black Hills.

The structure of the hills and surrounding plains was Winchell's chief concern. His lack of interest in gold dismayed Custer, who later would publicly criticize him for it, but Winchell stuck to what he believed was his assignment: the keeping of extensive notes on geological formations. "We go too fast," he complained in his journal, "for anything reliable in my line of investigation; indeed have always done so, except at great labor."

Newton Winchell was thirty-four years old and, although he was state geologist of Minnesota and a professor of geology at the University of Minnesota, he was not as well known as his older brother Alexander. Also a geologist, Alexander was chancellor of Syracuse University and was publishing this year a book on Darwinian theory. Newton had attended the University of Michigan while Alexander was professor of geology there, and after being graduated in 1866 with a strong interest in botany, archaeology, and geology, he had become a secondary schoolteacher for a while. Since 1872 he had held his dual post with the state of Minnesota.[12]

Although he despaired of making a significant contribution to geology in the time available, Winchell faithfully recorded everything of possible interest. Where streams had cut through the earth to reveal stratification, he described the strata in descending section. When he could he linked the formations with those universally recognized by geologists. "Dr. Hayden has mapped this as Fort Union

12. Biographies of both brothers appear in the *Dictionary of American Biography*. For Newton, see also *Who's Who in America*, 1899–1900.

Tertiary," he wrote of one formation, "but I am inclined to continue the Cretaceous as far west as this point, and to make the rock included in the foregoing section a lower portion of the Fox Hills group of Meek and Hayden with the upper part of the Fort Pierre."

The one opportunity he had to record an unusual geologic phenomenon, on the first leg of the expedition, proved to be an utter failure. This was the cave described in wondrous terms by Goose, the scout, and anxiously sought for by the whole command. Back at the fort, Goose had gone to Custer's quarters a few days before the start of the journey and fired the General's imagination with his tale of the marvelous cave. It was a gigantic place, Goose had said, filled with weird hieroglyphs, fossil bones, and certainly ghosts. On the reasonable assumption that Goose might indeed know of something notable in the cave line, Custer had put it on his agenda as a must.

On July 11 the General took a small detachment and broke off toward the ridge indicated by Goose as the location of the cave. There he found a hole washed out of the sandstone, two to three hundred feet long, with an entrance of fifteen by twenty feet, and of little interest either to scientists or curiosity-seekers. The walls bore a few markings, and near the entrance was a white man's skull which had apparently been pierced by a bullet.

No chambers, no grottoes, no crystals, no stalactites. One of the officers swore he could have dug a better cave in a week with a pick and shovel. General Forsyth listed it in his journal as a swindle, and Private Ewert called it "a rent in a cliff." Custer whimsically decided to call it Ludlow's Cave, but Colonel Ludlow could not bring himself to perpetuate the name. On the official chart of the expedition he simply listed it as "cave" (Figure 4).

A. B. DONALDSON

The contribution of Donaldson to the scientific end of the expedition appears slight. As botanist he made a small collection of plants which was sent for identification to Professor John M. Coulter, at Hanover, Indiana. Of the more than 1,000 plant species in the Black Hills, including 142 species of grasses, Donaldson collected only 75. It is entirely possible that he was not sponsored by the University of Minnesota, but by the St. Paul *Daily Pioneer* for which he wrote. This would explain his skimpy collecting and his long dispatches to the paper, but not the fact that he was described by everyone who mentioned him as the expedition's botanist. An ailing back hampered his botanizing during part of the trip.

Donaldson was forty-three years old, a native Ohioan who had been graduated from Ohio Wesleyan University and had taught for twenty years in Ohio schools. He loved to write, and his florid style was well suited to the journalism of the day. In 1875 he would buy the Alexandria, Minnesota, *Post* and publish it until his death in 1883.[13]

In the *Inter-Ocean,* Curtis called him "a big-bodied, big-hearted old fellow, a professor in a western college, who is doing the botany."

> His character [Curtis continued] is noble, yet funny, for in it are mixed the most generous, manly emotions, and a simple childishness it does one good to see. The professor—he alone, of the titled scientists, is exclu-

13. *South Dakota Historical Collections,* 7 (1914), 554n. Donaldson's dispatch of July 25, which first appeared in the *Daily Pioneer* of Aug. 15, 1874, is reprinted in this volume of the *Collections,* pp. 554–80.

sively known as such—is doing the botany; and to see
him come in from a long day's march, with a benevolent smile playing over his sun-burned, half-peeled face,
and wreathing itself in his whiskers, and a huge nosegay
of flowers in his hand—to see him lower his corpulent
form from the back of "Dobbin," slowly and carefully,
so as not to jar the sensitiveness of his rheumatic back,
and to hear his sigh of relief, breathed secretly under
a cheerful, hearty greeting, is as good as a tonic.[14]

WILLIAM H. ILLINGWORTH

Midafternoon, but still time to photograph the camp from
the bluff across the creek. The photographer hitched a team
to his spring wagon and set out for the highest point he
could find.

On a flat brow of sandstone too steep for a wagon to
mount, which he reached on foot with a tripod across his
shoulder, he set up his stereoscopic camera. He framed a
view that pleased him on the ground glass, after some
sweaty moments with a dark cloth swathed about his head,
then scrambled down to the wagon to prepare a plate.

In the wagon he carried a lightproof tent (which he
already had set up), several pounds each of collodion, iron
sulfate, potassium cyanide, silver nitrate, alcohol, nitric acid,
and varnish, a set of developing trays, a set of scales and
weights, and a box of glass squares far too fragile for so
much wagon transportation. He stepped inside the miserably
hot tent, and when he emerged a few minutes later he
carried in a light-tight plateholder a glass square which
he had treated with collodion and potassium iodide, then
immersed for several minutes in a bath of silver nitrate.

14. Curtis' dispatch of July 23 in the *Inter-Ocean* of Aug. 17, 1874.

This "wet plate," the basis of most of the photography of the period, had to be exposed and developed before the collodion turned dry in the low humidity of a July afternoon.

Up to the camera. Check the view. Insert the plate. Pull the slide carefully. Remove the lens cap for an exposure of, say, $f.32$ for ten or fifteen seconds. Then back to the airless tent for the developing. He poured a solution of ferrous sulfate over the plate to bring out the image, washed it in water to halt the process, and plunged it into a fixing bath of potassium cyanide. When the plate was washed and dried, William Illingworth had one more negative to protect from dust and breakage until he could get it back to his studio for printing.

Believing that photography was a little like magic, and immensely complicated, the soldiers of the expedition took all this rustle and clatter for granted. "Mr. Illingworth moved his camera to the top of the opposite bluff," one man wrote, "and stereoscoped us all."

Throughout the West, men for years had been removing lens caps, slowly counting to fifteen, and hoping that nobody moved. Exploring parties generally included a photographer who might be working jointly for himself and the government—hoping to profit from the sale of stereoscopic views to the public. S. N. Carvalho of Baltimore had been among the first, making daguerreotypes with John C. Frémont's fifth expedition at midcentury. In 1853, J. M. Stanley had made photographs with the I. I. Stevens party surveying for the railroad in the north. One of the best known of these pioneer craftsmen was W. H. Jackson, who traveled with Professor Hayden (and who would be coming through the Black Hills twenty-five years later to make views of the busy mining towns for a railroad company).

While Illingworth toiled in Prospect Valley, two other men were busy elsewhere. J. K. Hillers was with the J. W.

Powell expedition, touring the Rockies, and T. H. O'Sullivan was with the big Wheeler expedition surveying west of the 100th meridian.[15]

Illingworth got his first experience in photographing western scenes on the march when he accompanied the Fisk emigrant expedition in 1867, from St. Paul to Montana Territory. About thirty stereoscopic views of that venture were made by "Illingworth and Bill" and published by John Carbutt of Chicago. In 1867 Illingworth opened his own gallery in St. Paul; he was twenty-three at that time. He was born in England, brought to Philadelphia at an early age, and trained to help his father in the jewelry and clockmaking trade. He had lived in St. Paul since the early 1850s.[16]

When Colonel Ludlow engaged him to come with the Black Hills expedition, Illingworth may have been employed by another St. Paul photographer, Charles J. Huntington. The early newspaper stories reported that the photographs would be taken by "Huntington and Co.," and the published pictures later bore the imprint, "Published by Huntington & Winne, 60 West Third Street, Saint Paul."

Colonel Ludlow agreed to provide a camera and all the equipment, including a spring wagon, that had been used on the Yellowstone expedition. He agreed to provide rations, a horse and forage, plus enough money to meet all necessary living expenses. He would place Illingworth on the rolls as a teamster for pay purposes and provide an assistant if he needed one.

In return, Illingworth promised to deliver to Ludlow six

15. For information on early western photographers, see Robert Taft, *Photography and the American Scene* (New York, 1938), and a study of W. H. Jackson by W. J. Jackson, *Time Exposure* (New York, 1940).

16. T. M. Newsom, *Pen Pictures of St. Paul, Minnesota, and Biographical Sketches of Old Settlers* (St. Paul, 1886).

sets of the prints he obtained. He could keep the negatives for his own use.

Perhaps Illingworth has every intention of fulfilling his obligation as he lugs his big camera and his gloomy tent across the prairies. But he won't. He will give Ludlow one incomplete set of views, and when Ludlow complains he will say that he lacks the means to provide more. Yet, as Ludlow will note, he will be selling complete sets commercially through Huntington & Winne. Frustrated, Ludlow will try to prosecute him in the St. Paul courts for embezzlement of government property, and, failing on a technicality, will ask the War Department to take further action. The Judge Advocate General will decide against further proceedings, and all Ludlow will be able to do is comment publicly, in his official report, about Illingworth's defection.[17]

THE ENGINEERS

Sergeant Charles Becker was a solemn old German soldier who rode a two-wheeled odometer cart to measure the miles. On a terrible July day two years later, he would have the sad duty of riding that jouncy cart about the battlefield at the Little Big Horn, charting on paper the last hours of General Custer's command during the investigation of that disaster. Now he was simply charting his way to the Black Hills, and this assignment made him a much-sought-after man. The first question the soldiers asked when camp was made: How many miles today? If Becker's horse had

17. Ludlow's difficulties with Illingworth are set forth in Ludlow to Chief of Engineers, Jan. 12, 1875, LR, Chief of Engineers, No. 125 (1875), RG 77, NA. The letter bears endorsements by the Secretary of War and the Judge Advocate General.

not run away during the march and fouled up his calculations, he could give the answer to the last tenth of a mile.

Following a different trail, but roughly paralleling the
route of Sergeant Becker, was another engineer in an ambulance also carrying odometers. An odometer was an instru-
ment in a stout leather case, strapped to the wheel of a
cart to measure the revolutions. At night the readings of the
instruments were averaged and converted to miles. If the
route had been level, no correction factor was applied; if
the country had been rough the reading was reduced from
1 to 3 per cent.

Becker and another sergeant carried prismatic compasses
and kept a full record of compass readings. When these
distances and directions were committed to paper, the result
was a "meander line," the simplest kind of mapping tech-
nique. When checked against astronomical observations for
latitude and longitude, and augmented by barometric readings for altitude, these calculations became the raw material
for the maps that Becker would draw when he got back to
the drafting room in Department headquarters at St. Paul.

Each sergeant had an assistant to help with compass readings. A fifth man carried two chronometers in a basket to
minimize jarring, and the sixth member of the detachment
was equipped with a thermometer and aneroid barometer.
Besides these enlisted soldiers there was a civilian topogra-
pher, W. H. Wood, who helped Colonel Ludlow with
transit and sextant readings during the day, and made night
observations whenever practical.

Obviously, Colonel Ludlow was not conducting a sophisticated topographic survey; he knew that his work must be
done over by men with more time and better equipment.
He was meticulous, however. The position of most of the
camps he determined astronomically. Now that he was in
rougher country, where points of reference were available,

he was doing some triangulation—checking points in the hills from a measured base by means of trigonometry. But mathematics and the tricky workings of the aneroid barometer would lead him astray at least once. He would record the altitude of Harney's Peak as 9,700 feet, a mark some 2,500 feet higher than later measurements.

The records of Ludlow's observations are still on file, with a manuscript copy of his final report, in the National Archives. He made his calculations on printed forms, ruled off with thin red and blue lines and bearing such headings as "Determination of the Latitude by the Observed Double Altitudes of Polaris off the Meridian."

Although he was not considered a fighting soldier, and was classed with the bug hunters by the troops, Ludlow had the respect of the line officers. He was, as Samuel Barrows said, "an engineer who was not afraid of getting sunburnt." He had known Barrows and most of the Seventh Cavalry officers since the Yellowstone expedition, when he had surveyed the Yellowstone River from its mouth at Fort Buford to a point ten miles above the Powder River.

Ludlow was thirty-one, the son of distinguished Civil War general William Handy Ludlow. He was a West Pointer, class of '64, and as chief engineer of the XX Corps he had been breveted three times for gallantry during the war. A long career lay ahead. Eventually he would command a brigade in the Spanish-American War and serve for a time as military governor of Havana.[18]

18. Col. Ludlow's published report is the source of the brief facts about his surveying operations. A typed copy of the recollections of W. H. Wood, including his work with Ludlow, is owned by the State Historical Society of North Dakota. For biographical accounts of Ludlow, see the *Dictionary of American Biography* and Thomas H. S. Hamersly, *Complete Regular Army Register of the United States* (Washington, 1880).

THE MEDICS

When the expedition pulled out of Prospect Valley in the early dawn of July 16, Custer took some extra measures to protect the train against Indians. Signal smokes had been seen. Both Bloody Knife and Goose suspected there might be a war party ahead on the Little Missouri (but there was not). An extra company from each battalion was detailed to march ahead of the column, with the pioneer corps, and the commanders of the two flanking battalions were warned not to let the wagon train fall behind.

There was an alarm in the morning when Charley Reynolds dashed up to Colonel Tilford and reported a party of Indians on the left. The flankers reported a body of men also, moving about two miles from the column and in the same direction. Reynolds raced ahead to warn Custer, the company commanders were cautioned to be vigilant, and the column moved tensely ahead until the obvious fact sank in: the party that Reynolds and the flankers had sighted was Lieutenant Benjamin Hodgson of Company B, scouting the Short Pine Hills with a party of scientists and reporters.[19]

The expedition was in Montana Territory now, and would be there for the next two days. The 104th meridian lay a few miles west of the last campsite. In the afternoon some water was found at a bend of the Little Missouri, a rapid stream thirty to forty feet wide and eighteen inches deep, flowing over a gravelly bed. There also was plenty of wood but not a spear of grass for the livestock. So the men filled the kegs, tossed dry cottonwood onto the wagons, and marched on. It was 9 P.M. before they found grass, after a dirty march of thirty-odd miles. The soldiers were irritable. Some of the troopers in Company H thought they were being

19. Several scientists and reporters mention the scout to the Short Pine Hills, but the Indian alarm is recorded only in Ewert's journal.

crowded by G and M on either side, when picketing their horses, so they began to pull picket pins and clear the way for their own mounts. Quarrels followed, supper was late, no tents were raised, and the day that had begun in the soft grasses of Prospect Valley now ended in the gritty wastes —with everyone feeling thoroughly miserable.

While many men had been injured or indisposed on the trip, particularly in the first few days, few had been seriously ill. The physicians accompanying the train had kept themselves busy administering treatment for diarrhea and bandaging the inevitable wounds. Now they found a case to test their skills in the affliction of John Cunningham.

For a week or so, Private Cunningham of Company H had been feeling poorly. He had tried once to go on sick report but the medical officer, believing that his diarrhea was not serious and certainly not unique in the command, had ordered him back to duty. Cunningham stayed in the saddle during the march of July 17, growing weaker and finding it harder to mount after the rest periods. The trail led south over rolling prairie and scant grass. It may have cheered Cunningham a little to catch a first glimpse of the Black Hills in midmorning, but there were still many miles of aching, numbing travel between him and those cool ranges.

Camp on the 17th was made in Wyoming Territory, at the edge of a bluff facing south, overlooking the rough country they faced tomorrow. The Hills were now in full view beyond that hellish foreground, and most of the men felt that the worst of their trip was over. Private Cunningham did not. He turned himself in to his first sergeant once more and was taken to the medical officer. Again he was returned to duty.

In the night a storm blew down many tents and the march of July 18 began with wet clothing and ill humor.

By noon they had reached a branch of the Belle Fourche and found a bit of burr oak and pine; a few miles more brought them to the rim of the Belle Fourche Valley, where two or three hours were spent looking for a way to get the wagons down past the scarred, timbered slopes. At last they were in the valley where the Belle Fourche ran fast and clear.

Private Cunningham got a lucky break when Custer decided to keep the command in camp July 19 because of rain. But the rest did not help him much, and during the march of July 20 he collapsed and fell from his horse. Convinced at last, the medical officer placed him on sick report and assigned him to ride in an ambulance, and now he became the subject of an impassioned outburst in the journal of Private Ewert.

Throughout the expedition, Ewert had been bothered by Custer's use of "the best ambulance" for his natural-history collection.[20] Ewert claimed that this was the newest vehicle in the command, providing more comfort than the other rickety contraptions with broken springs. He also was angry because the large tent intended for hospital use was employed by Custer as a dining room for his staff. "Whether it was intended for this use by the government, or whether it was issued for the accommodation of the sick is left to the judgment of the reader."

Medical duties of the expedition were divided among three physicians. Dr. A. C. Bergen, of Vinton, Iowa, was assigned to the infantry battalion. Dr. S. J. Allen, Jr., was assigned to the left cavalry battalion which contained the Com-

20. The driver of the ambulance in which Custer carried his specimens of flora and fauna was Fred S. Snow. His recollections are contained in a manuscript, "Black Hills Expedition, 1874," package 31, E. B. Custer Collection, Custer Battlefield National Monument, Crow Agency, Montana.

pany H of Privates Cunningham and Ewert. Captain J. W. Williams, from Fort Rice, handled the medical problems of the right battalion and was also chief medical officer of the command. Williams was a Mississippian, a graduate of the National Medical College in Washington, and had been active throughout the Civil War—serving in 1864–65, for example, as surgeon-in-chief with the First Cavalry Division of the Army of the Shenandoah.[21]

The story of Captain Williams' handling of Private Cunningham is told by Ewert, with the prejudice and exaggeration that might be expected from the pen of a worried comrade. He said he went around to visit Cunningham in the ambulance, and was told by another sick trooper that no physician had visited either of them since the previous evening. Ewert then went to the tent of Captain Williams and found him "lying on his bed, in a drunken sleep." He then went to the adjutant, Lieutenant Calhoun, and begged him to help Cunningham. Calhoun immediately went to the physician's tent and awoke him "with great effort." Then, said Ewert, Williams staggered over to the ambulance, "looked at the dying man for a moment with a drunken stare, then staggered back to his tent, fell on his bed—and slept." Ewert finally reached Custer through Professor Donaldson, and Custer ordered Dr. Allen to attend Cunningham. But it was too late, and the trooper died near midnight, "purely through the neglect of the men claiming to be doctors, men who were paid by the Government to look after the health of its soldiers and who only managed to drink the brandy furnished by the same government for the use of its sick soldiers."[22]

21. Biographical notes on Williams are in drawer 812, Medical Officers' Personal Files, RG 94, NA.
22. Ewert, pp. 24–26.

Captain Williams may indeed have been drunk, but he had other problems, also. During the next several years he served in a succession of posts from Walla Walla, Washington, to the Atlantic seaboard. When he fell ill and died in the spring of 1889, the attending physician said that apparently he was a narcotics addict. "I am of the opinion that he had been habitually addicted to the excessive use of chloral hydrate and chloroform—and that the brain and nervous system had been gradually failing in vital capacity for a long period."[23]

During the last two days of Cunningham's illness, the column had penetrated the Black Hills. The blue mists which for days had clung to the horizon finally became massive, forested mountains. The first day's journey into the region, July 20, had been hard on the wagons but delightful for the cavalrymen. Crossing the Belle Fourche and heading west, they had moved from the dry, burned-up landscape north of the river to a place where the air was sweet and the grass knee-deep. On the 21st they descended the valley of the Red Water, a branch of the Belle Fourche, and camped at a spring where the temperature of the water was 45 degrees. It was here that Cunningham had died.

On the morning of July 22, when the body of the dead trooper had been wrapped in canvas and laid in an ambulance, and the men were at the picket line saddling their horses, the sound of gunfire snapped across the valley. When soldiers from the adjoining companies rushed to the Company M picket line, they found Private George Turner writhing with a bullet wound in the abdomen. He had been shot by Private William Roller.

Turner and Roller had quarreled for years, their comrades said. When at last they had drawn upon each other, Turner

23. Report of Maj. Harvey E. Brown, April 22, 1889, in Williams' personal file, NA.

was momentarily confused because he was not wearing his holster in its normal position. During his delay in getting hold of his pistol he was shot at close range by Roller. It then developed that the men had argued because Turner had cross-hobbled Roller's horse—crossing the sideline from the left forefoot to the right hindfoot so that the animal could not walk without falling.

Turner got a curt epitaph in Private Ewert's journal: "The men in his company expressed no sympathy, he having but few friends."[24] Captain Williams performed an autopsy on the dead man, and the Arikara scouts told their own version of that procedure many years later:

> Their interpreter told them that two soldiers were quarreling and one of them asked Custer for permission to finish the fight. Custer said, "I don't care," and one of the soldiers got his gun out. The scouts heard someone call, "Hold on, hold on," and then a shot, and then another. The soldier shot his comrade through the arm and then through the heart. . . . Custer came to the scouts and told them that the doctor was planning to cut up the body to see why he was so quarrelsome. The scouts saw the doctor cut the body open, put salt in the body, put all the parts back and then the body was buried.[25]

Now there were two corpses to carry along in the ambulance. The column set a course southward, up the Red Water, following a heavily marked Indian trail that apparently led to the Red Cloud and Spotted Tail agencies. The command

24. Most of the story of the murder is based on Ewert's account.
25. Alfred Bear, "Story Told by Strikes Two and Bear's Belly of an Expedition Under Custer to the Black Hills in June, 1875 [July, 1874]," *North Dakota Historical Collections*, 6 (1920), 163–75.

went into camp on Inyan Kara Creek and prepared for the burial of the men.

A double grave was dug upon a small knoll, and in the evening the regiment fell into line by companies to attend the service. No chaplain had come with the expedition, for there was none stationed either at Fort Lincoln or Fort Rice, and the Episcopal service was read by Irish sergeant Michael Walsh of Company H. Afterward, a fire was burned upon the grave to camouflage the site from the Indians.

It was a time for the kind of prose that came so handily to the pen of Professor Donaldson. "A thousand thoughts come crowding up for utterance," he wrote, "but we forbear, and leave the reader to moralize upon this painful drama of real life."[26]

26. Donaldson's dispatch of July 25 in the *Daily Pioneer* of Aug. 15, 1874.

CHAPTER 4

The New El Dorado

July 23 to August 3

On a summit in Wyoming, the highest point of land that Custer had ever stood upon, he watched Colonel Ludlow working with hammer and chisel. When the Colonel stepped back to inspect his work, he had created a monument. The inscription read:

'74
CUSTER

A mountain called Inyan Kara was the place. On the morning of July 23, Custer brought his scientific team and two companies of cavalry to the base of the mountain, four miles from camp. Leaving the cavalry escort to wait there, he climbed with Ludlow, Donaldson, and a few others to an altitude of 6,500 feet.

While the General was climbing, correspondent Curtis stayed in camp and wrote a dispatch for the *Inter-Ocean* that was skeptical. "So far we have seen nothing remarkable; the miners have discovered no gold; the geologists have whacked in vain for the fossil of the 'missing link'; the naturalists have emptied their saddle pockets day after day without revealing the existence of any new wonders in life; the soldiers have fought no Indians, and so far the expedition, in a positive sense, has been unsuccessful."[1]

1. Curtis' dispatch of July 23 in the *Inter-Ocean* of Aug. 10, 1874.

1. The expedition enters the Black Hills via the Red Water Valley.

2. Camp from which Custer climbed Inyan Kara mountain.

3. The column ascends Floral Valley and crosses into Castle Creek Valley.

4. Location of the small Indian camp, headed by Chief One Stab.

5. Discovery of gold in Custer Park on French Creek.

6. Custer makes a scout to the south with five companies.

7. Scout Charles Reynolds departs for Laramie with news of the gold strike.

8. Colonels Hart and Ludlow take two companies on a scout of French Creek.

9. Custer kills his first grizzly bear.

10. The command leaves the Hills and heads for home.

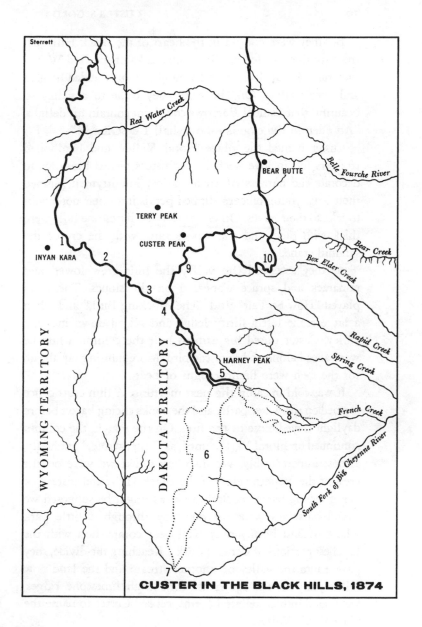

Sterrett

Red Water Creek

Belle Fourche River

BEAR BUTTE

TERRY PEAK

CUSTER PEAK

Bear Creek

INYAN KARA

Box Elder Creek

1

2

3

4

5

6

7

8

9

10

WYOMING TERRITORY

DAKOTA TERRITORY

HARNEY PEAK

Rapid Creek

Spring Creek

French Creek

South Fork of Big Cheyenne River

CUSTER IN THE BLACK HILLS, 1874

But they were not yet in the heart of the Black Hills. On the 24th the trail led up the steep banks of the Red Water, then turned sharply east and wound among wooded heights and open valleys. On the 25th they came to a valley so beautiful that Samuel Barrows could not contain his delight. "An Eden in the clouds—how shall I describe it!"

Custer named the place Floral Valley, and hardboiled troopers fell in love with it. Teamsters picked blossoms to decorate the harness of their mules; infantrymen plumed their hats; young officers slipped petals into their notebooks to take to their wives. On either side the limestone hills were thick with pine, and the woods rang with the cry of the sandhill crane.

As they ascended the valley the hills grew lower, and tamarack and spruce appeared on the slopes. The band played "How So Fair" and "The Mocking Bird," and when a large crane left a flinty ledge and glided down into the valley, Custer raised his arm to halt the column while he went ahead alone and shot the bird. More hunting lay ahead, for the men were finding signs of bear.

It was cold in camp the next morning. A thin crust of ice formed on the water pails, and the cooks slicing bacon before daylight stayed close to the fires. On the march, the column continued up Floral Valley until, as Custer wrote, "gradually, almost imperceptibly, we discovered that we were on the crest of the western ridge of the Black Hills, and instead of being among barren rockey peaks as might be supposed we found ourselves wending our way through a little park whose natural beauty may well bear comparison with the loveliest portions of Central Park." Reaching the divide, they passed into the valley of another stream and the land now fell rapidly to the southeast. The high limestone ridges, weathered into castellated forms, caused Custer to name the place Castle Valley.

And here he found his Indians. A teen-aged Arikara scout named Little Hawk made the discovery; a detachment of scouts had found a camp with the fires still smoldering, and Custer ordered them on down the valley to look around. Little Hawk (according to Curtis in the *Inter-Ocean*) then came upon five Sioux lodges, and word was sent back to Custer. Taking Company E, the General hustled down to a wooded ravine where some of his scouts had hidden themselves to wait for him. Here he was joined by Company C and the rest of the excited scouts, and they carefully maneuvered themselves closer to the camp.

Next he sent interpreter Louis Agard and a couple of Sioux scouts into the camp with a flag of truce, to announce his presence and assure the startled Indians that he meant no harm. By now the campers were aware of his presence, and he had galloped his detachment in a wide circle and surrounded the five lodges. As soon as Agard had explained the situation to the Indians, Custer dismounted, came forward, and shook hands with a brave named Slow Bull. "How! How!" he said in the universal way, and his grin was enough to calm the men. Some of the women and children, however, were sorely frightened.

Slow Bull sent some of the older children to call in One Stab, chief of the band, who was hunting at a nearby deer lick with three other men. Then he began to answer the questions of Custer's interpreters. They were Oglalas, he said, twenty-seven souls in all, who had been in the Hills for two months. He claimed they were attached to both agencies down in Nebraska—Red Cloud's and Spotted Tail's —and that no word of the expedition had reached them.

Slow Bull was a tall, slim warrior with sharp features and piercing dark eyes, and his wife was the daughter of Red Cloud. While they talked the wife brought cold water from a spring in an old iron kettle. Samuel Barrows described her for his *Tribune* readers.

> A not uncomely squaw she was, with a broad full face and a straight nose, a little hooked at the end, long black hair braided into a pair of "tails," dark, bright eyes, and a fine set of teeth, which just then were composedly chewing the gum of the pine tree. Mrs. Red Cloud–Slow Bull had with her neighbor squaws been very much frightened at first, but she had now recovered and was so glad that her husband and little ones were not going to be killed that she became very agreeable, and entertained us in a most lively manner. Her teepee was the cleanest and neatest of the five; in fact one of the few Indian teepees that invite an entrance. The family effects, such as were not needed for immediate use, were packed up in clean skins tied with thongs and disposed around the tent. Other skins were spread on the ground to lie upon. In one corner was a long dress or gown of buckskin, completely covered with beads, the evidence of great industry as well as vanity. Mrs. R. C. Slow Bull had given a pony for it.

When she told Custer she had no coffee or sugar and that her children were hungry, he promised her food. During the parley a small dog came into the lodge, sat down in the middle of the crowd, scratched itself and went to sleep.

To the obvious relief of the tense Indians, their chief arrived. Not with a flourish, however, for One Stab was less than prepossessing. He was an old man in a weatherbeaten felt hat, a breech clout, a dirty cotton shirt, and muddy moccasins. But he also wore the mantle of authority, for he was chief of eighty Oglala lodges. He smoked a peace pipe

with Custer and the two men discussed the topography of
the Hills.

What Custer wanted from these people was information.
His maps were no longer adequate and his guides knew almost nothing about the Hills. If Custer could calm the
apprehensions of these nomads and load them down with
bacon and sugar, they might prove useful.

The General himself relates what happened next:

> Later in the afternoon four of the men including the
> Chief "One Stab" visited our camp and desired the
> promised rations, saying the entire party would come
> up and favor us. The following morning as agreed
> upon, I ordered presents of Sugar, Coffee and bacon
> to be given them and to relieve them of their pretended
> anxiety for the safety of their village during the night,
> I ordered a party of fifteen of my command to return
> with them and protect them during the night. But
> from their great disinclinations to wait a few moments
> until the party could saddle up and from the fact that
> two of the four had already slipped away I was of the
> opinion that they were not actually [acting] in good
> faith in this. I was confirmed when the two remaining
> ones set off at a gallop in the direction of the village.
> I sent a party of men (Scouts) to overtake them and
> requested their return, not complying with the request
> I sent a second party with orders to repeat the request
> and if not complied with to take hold of the bridles of
> their ponies and lead them back but to offer no violence;
> when overtaken by our scouts one of the two included
> seized the musket of one of the scouts and endeavored
> to wrest it from him, failing in this he released his
> hold after the scout became dismounted in the struggle
> and set off as fast as his pony could carry him but not

before the musket of the scout was discharged. From
blood discovered afterwards, it was evident that either
the Indian or his pony was wounded. I hope that
neither was seriously hurt although the Indians had
thus their bad faith as the sole ground for the collision.

According to the dispatch written by Barrows, the shooting of the fleeing Indian was not accidental. He said the
Santee scout who was involved in the scuffle dropped off his
horse, took aim, and fired. Something seems to have frightened these Indians even after Custer's friendly approach had
won them over. Perhaps the answer lies in Private Ewert's
journal. Ewert said the Arikaras had painted themselves
and stripped for war when the camp was found, and that
they pleaded with Custer for the privilege of killing the
Sioux. Throughout the whole episode they were difficult to
control and they may finally have convinced the Sioux that
they planned to kill them.

The scouts went on down to the camp and found it
abandoned. The fleeing women had destroyed all the camp
equipage they could not carry, chopped up their lodgepoles,
cut holes in their kettles, and discarded their jerked meat.
The scouts followed their trail for some time, but they had
gone too far to be overtaken.

One Stab was still in camp, either as guest or captive—
depending on one's point of view. Custer wrote, perhaps
with tongue in cheek, "I have effected arrangements by
which the Chief One Stab remains with us as a guide."
William Curtis said that the old man, claiming surprise at
the escape of his people, "was told that he would be kept
a hostage until we were out of the Hills, and must show us
a good road."

An even bleaker picture was drawn by the Arikara scouts
in their narrative of the expedition. They said that old One

Illustrations

Fig. 1. Passing in single column through Castle Creek Valley, the wagon train is two miles long.

Fig. 2. In camp at Hiddenwood Creek, with the wagon train parked inside a hollow square of tents.

Fig. 3. Photographer William Illingworth called this view "Our First Crossing of an Alkali Valley."

Fig. 4. Ludlow's Cave, named for the expedition's engineering officer, was over-sold by a Sioux scout named Goose and became an object of ridicule when the column reached it.

Fig. 5. Inyan Kara, a mountain climbed by Custer (p. 75). Shadow in the foreground is of Illingworth, peering into the ground glass of his camera.

Fig. 6. The permanent camp at Custer's Gulch from which most of the gold prospecting was done.

Fig. 7. Perhaps this is the champagne supper mentioned by Private Ewert (p. 84), given by Colonel Tilford while Custer was away from camp. The men are not identified.

Fig. 8. Near Harney's Peak the photographer caught this scene; he named the place "Illingworth Valley" in honor of himself.

Fig. 9. The photographer identified this man as "our wagon master." The wagon-master or trainmaster of the expedition was Michael Smith.

Fig. 10. Custer has achieved a lifelong ambition, the shooting of a grizzly. Left to right: Bloody Knife, an Arikara scout; General Custer; Private Noonan, the General's orderly; and Lieutenant Colonel William Ludlow, Corps of Engineers.

Fig. 11. Trying to stand motionless while photographer Illingworth operates his slow camera, the expedition is drawn up in customary marching order. Note several civilians in the foreground, riding mules.

Fig. 12. The inevitable group photograph, showing all the officers and scientists in front of the headquarters tent.

Stab was tied to an iron picket pin, and that his feet were hobbled. "The Dakota captive cried in the night and by signs said that his children would cut their hair as for his death since he was as good as dead."

Hobbled he may have been, but he was not injured. He would stay a few days with Custer, guiding him on a trip into the southern Hills. The other Indians who had fled would hasten back to the agencies and announce that One Stab had been killed, and there would be angry talk among the Oglalas, but then the old man would go free.[2]

A Black Hills myth had been shattered; the place was not teeming with hostiles. So Custer turned to another legend and pursued it as vigorously as he had ever pursued a band of warriors. He began to look for gold.

THE FIRST COLOR

The excitement started when miners Horatio N. Ross and William McKay began to run across the right kind of potentially gold-bearing quartz. From the moment they had entered the Hills they had prospected diligently, rumbling their wagon up one valley and down another, probing the creek beds. Tradition was on their side, and the quartz looked mighty good.

If Ross and McKay were officially attached to the command, nobody ever admitted it. In the eyes of the world they were just "with" Custer. Barrows covered the subject by saying that the two men furnished their own team, wagon,

2. The preceding story of the encounter with One Stab is drawn from Custer to Sheridan, Aug. 2, 1874, in Custer's order and dispatch book; Barrows' dispatch of July 28 in the *Tribune* of Aug. 18, 1874; Curtis' dispatch of July 27 in the *Inter-Ocean* of Aug. 18, 1874; Donaldson's dispatch of July 25 in the *Daily Pioneer* of Aug. 15, 1874; and Col. Ludlow's report, the Arikara narrative, and the journal of Pvt. Ewert.

and equipment, and were at liberty to prospect wherever they chose. Teamster Fred Snow, half a century later, would recall that Custer financed them himself. This might have involved nothing more than the cost of rations.

Ross and McKay were experienced miners and trusted frontiersmen. Ross had once been in charge of a high-producing gold mine at Gregory Point, Colorado. McKay, an early settler near Fort Randall, was a member of the Dakota territorial legislature. As the men of the regiment watched these two searching, crouching at streamside with their shovels and pans, the gold fever grew.

On July 27 the expedition remained in Castle Valley camp to explore and prospect. Several surveying parties toured the tributary valleys where grass was as high as a horse's shoulder. Companies F and H were out all day, and Company H logged twenty-four miles with the miners but found no gold. In Castle Valley it almost invariably grew cloudy in the afternoon, interfering with Ludlow's astronomical observations and bringing a drop in temperature.

On the next day Custer relied too heavily on an Indian guide, and an interpreter who misunderstood the guide's advice, and marched his command five miles east to an impasse. The column wheeled and made a second camp on Castle Creek, just two miles below the previous one.

After a difficult march on July 29, the expedition spent July 30 rolling through a rich land, half wood and half glade. Riding ahead, Custer found it first. Professor Donaldson made his one and only comment about Custer's vanity: "After much entreaty, his modesty as far gave way as reluctantly to consent to the request of the topographical engineer that the name be Custer Park."

Now they were near the outer plains on the east side of the Hills. The air was milder and the grass crisper, the streams skimpier. A few grasshoppers reminded them of the rough days facing them on the homeward march. About noon, the column stopped to rest approximately ten miles from Harney's Peak, the highest point in the Hills. One of the miners, probably Ross, took his pan and went to the creek to perform the ritual that was now familiar to every man in the command. When he had washed a couple of panfuls of earth, he found a few glittering grains—pinpoints of gold.

The word did not spread rapidly. The miner wrapped the golden flecks in a bit of paper, and that night by the glow of a lantern in Custer's tent, some of the officers and scientists studied it hopefully. It was only "color," the kind of gold you could wash out of any western stream with a bit of luck. Barrows said the news of the find created less excitement than the discovery of Floral Valley—perhaps because the men were still skeptical.[3]

GOLD AT THE GRASS ROOTS

The command stayed in camp the next day. The miners went out early to improve on yesterday's panning and Custer set out to climb Harney's Peak. The enlisted men organized a baseball game. All three projects were successful.

Ross and McKay found a bar that yielded five to seven cents per pan. It would pay out if water were a bit more plentiful but it was not exactly the big strike they wanted. They kept on looking, certain now they had found what the correspondents called "The New El Dorado."

Custer and an escort commanded by Lieutenant Varnum reached the foot of Harney's Peak after a rough ride through heavily timbered ravines. They climbed the old granite crag to what Colonel Ludlow thought was an altitude of 9,700 feet (it was really 7,200) and sighted two other high peaks

3. For the details of the gold discovery I rely mainly on Barrows' dispatch of Aug. 10 in the *Tribune* of Aug. 28, 1874.

which they named for General Terry and General Custer. "The return to camp," Ludlow wrote, "was a struggle against almost every possible obstacle—rocks, creeks, marshes, willow and aspen thickets, pine timber, dead and fallen trees, steep hillsides and precipitous ravines."[4] It was after midnight when they reached camp after some stalwart guidance by Lieutenant Varnum, and the worried officers in camp had built signal fires to lead them in.

Perhaps the ballgame was the most successful of all the day's activities. Conscious of history, Private Ewert carefully noted that it was the first such game ever played in the Black Hills. One team, the Actives of Fort Lincoln, was picked from members of the band and the right wing; the other team, the Athletes of Fort Rice, included men from Companies C, H, and K. Umpire was John Tempany, whom Ewert called "Mr. Tenpenny, Vetinary Surgeon," and he allegedly favored the Fort Lincoln team. It was evident to every spectator that he was partial, Ewert said, but the Athletes finished the game without a murmur. Score: Actives 11, Athletes 6.

After the game, Colonel Tilford stretched a tarpaulin between two trees and gave a champagne supper (Figure 7) for some of the officers. (Ewert said that Fred Grant was "one of the boozy ones" at this party.) When the Company H glee club went over to serenade the group, Lieutenant McDougall took them to the tent of Samuel Barrows where they sang "Come Where My Love Lies Dreaming," "Dinah's Wedding," "The Vacant Chair," and "Under the Willows." Barrows repaid them with two bottles of whiskey.[5]

The next day, August 1, the camp was moved three miles for better grazing. Custer named the site Agnes Park to honor Agnes Bates, a friend of Elizabeth's. His announce-

4. Ludlow, p. 14.
5. Ewert, pp. 37–38.

ment that a mail would leave within thirty-six hours set many of the soldiers to writing letters, and others caught hundreds of fish in the creek.

Here the miners found excellent colors in the loose soil along the creek, so they sank a hole in the most promising bar. When they had dug down six feet the water seepage impeded their work, and they quit before reaching bedrock. They estimated that the earth would pan out as high as ten cents.

Ten cents a pan in loose diggings could mean more than a dollar a pan where the going was more difficult. If conditions were right a miner might shovel 1,500 pans of earth into a sluice in a day, bringing him $150 at ten cents a pan. But Ross said he doubted if the gold at this place (they were calling it Custer Gulch now) would yield more than $50 or $75 a day.

Everyone was prospecting, using shovels, picks, tent pins, pothooks, bowie knives, mess pans, plates, and tin cups. Sarah Campbell, the Negro cook who worked for sutler John Smith, was an excited prospector. The men called her Aunt Sally and she called herself "the only white woman that ever saw the Black Hills."[6]

THE MIDNIGHT RIDE OF CHARLEY REYNOLDS

Government scout Charles Reynolds will accompany the five companies of cavalry which leave camp tomorrow morning and at a point hereafter to be designated will proceed with dispatches to Fort Laramie reporting his arrival to the commanding officer of that post.

On arrival he will deposit in the mail such dispatches and letters as are intended for transmission by

6. Curtis' dispatch of Aug. 7 in the *Inter-Ocean* of Aug. 27, 1874.

mail and should there be a telegraph station at Fort
Laramie he will deliver to the operator such dispatches
as may be intended for telegraph. Should there be no
telegraph at Fort Laramie he will proceed to the nearest
telegraph station, taking with him all mail and telegraph matter consigned to his care. On completing
this duty he will proceed to Fort Lincoln and await
the arrival of this command.

Upon arrival at Fort Laramie he will turn in the
public horse ridden by him to the post quartermaster
at Fort Laramie, which officer is requested to receipt
for the same.[7]

A predictable legend grew out of Reynolds' dash to
Fort Laramie. Old-timers say that Custer called for a volun-
teer to carry news of the strike to the nearest telegraph station. A long pause, a tense moment while lesser men lowered
their eyes, and then the lone voice. "I'll go, General. I'll go."

Charley Reynolds volunteered, to be sure, but he did it
the day he signed on at Fort Lincoln. It had been planned
from the beginning that he would carry a mail out of the
Hills if circumstances warranted, just as he had done the
year before on the Yellowstone expedition. At that time he
and a fellow scout had ridden from the Musselshell to Fort
Benton, about 150 miles, without starting a legend.

Custer was going to make two deep probes into the southern Hills. He would take five companies on a rapid scout to
the South Fork of the Cheyenne, and Reynolds would go
along, continuing by himself beyond the river. Another small
reconnaissance would be launched toward the southeast to
do some additional mapping. The smaller group would con-
sist of two companies of cavalry, Louis Agard, Winchell,
and Grinnell, and a mapping team under Lieutenant God-

7. Custer's Special Order No. 26, Aug. 2, 1874.

frey. They would take no wagons but would carry their supplies on pack mules. Because of the tortuous, deepset nature of the stream they followed, they would fail to reach the Cheyenne.

Custer took the whole right battalion with him, with Colonel Ludlow along to do the mapping, and with bedding, forage, and food loaded on pack mules. The trail took them south and southwest through the mellow park country until they reached the head of a creek flowing southwest; they followed the creek all day, entering a narrow valley that grew broader as they advanced. The hills grew lower and the timber thinned out. After marching forty-five miles they camped for the night a few miles from the Cheyenne. Then Custer added the final touches to the packet of mail he had prepared.

His long report to Sheridan had been written back at the main camp. Its final lines told of the discovery.

> As there are scientists accompanying the expedition who are examining into the mineral resources of this region, the result of whose researches will accompany my detailed report, I omit all present reference to that portion of our explorations until the return of the expedition, except to state, what will appear in any event in the public prints, that gold has been found in several places, and it is the belief of those who are giving their attention to this subject that it will be found in paying quantities. I have upon my table 40 or 50 small particles of pure gold, in size averaging that of a small pin head, and most of it obtained today from one panful of earth. As we have never remained longer at our camp than one day, it will be readily understood that there is no opportunity to make a satisfactory examination in regard to deposits of valuable minerals.

Veins of lead and strong indications of the existence
of silver have been found. Until further examination
is made regarding the richness of gold, no opinion
should be formed.[8]

It took Charley Reynolds four nights to travel the ninety
miles to Fort Laramie. The risk was heightened by the fact
that his course intersected several Indian trails at right
angles, where he might come upon a band of hostiles un-
expectedly. Mrs. Custer, who later told the story and may
have touched it up a bit, said he sometimes heard Indian
voices as he lay hidden during the day. Finally he had to
walk and lead his exhausted horse, she said, while suffering
from thirst. When he reached Fort Laramie his tongue and
lips were so swollen he could not close his mouth.[9]

To military men in the West, sending a dispatch across
the wilds in Charley Reynolds' mailbag was almost as safe
as filing it with a telegraph operator. He was such a contrast
to the prototype of the western scout—the tobacco-chewing,
guffawing old loudmouth—that his pleasantly surprised
associates made a fuss over him. He was the quiet, blue-eyed
gentleman in buckskin. Barrows said he was "simple and
reticent in speech, yet no trace of western braggadocio, ruf-
fianism, or ill-nature." Curtis, ever effusive when he met a
clean-collared Westerner, insisted that Reynolds might
adorn a drawing room "if it wasn't for his diffidence." Curtis
said Charley was born and raised in Kentucky (other sources
say Warren County, Illinois), and that he was "a short,
stocky man, with a shrinking blue eye, and a face from which
exposure has not yet effaced the beauty, a voice as soft as
a woman's, and a manner unobtrusive and gentle."[10]

8. Custer's official dispatch of Aug. 2, 1874.
9. *Boots and Saddles*, pp. 240–41.
10. Barrows' dispatch of July 8 in the *Tribune* of Aug. 1, and Curtis'
dispatch of Aug. 3 in the *Inter-Ocean* of Aug. 27, 1874.

By August 13 Reynolds had performed his assignment and reached Sioux City, where he was pounced upon by news-hungry citizens. He gave the editor of the Sioux City *Journal* a mildly enthusiastic review of the gold situation, saying in answer to the inevitable question that he had not personally picked up any nuggets. In fact he knew of no one else who had, but he had seen gold washed from surface dirt yielding two or three cents a pan. Having delivered this restrained appraisal of the strike, he set out for Bismarck.[11]

Charley's less than frantic attitude toward the gold potential of the Hills, and Custer's warning that no conclusions could be drawn until all the facts were in, put no damper on the enthusiasm of the frontier townsmen. The dispatches from Barrows, Curtis, and Knappen had already triggered the celebration. Knappen set the tone for newspaper reports in the Bismarck *Tribune* of August 12. "Here, in Custer's Valley, rich gold and silver mines have been discovered, both placer and quartz diggings; and this immense section, bids fair to become the El Dorado of America."

The Yankton *Press and Dakotaian* broke the news on August 13 with this headline:

STRUCK IT AT LAST!

Rich Mines of Gold and Silver
Reported Found by Custer

PREPARE FOR LIVELY TIMES!

Gold Expected to Fall 10 per Cent.—
Spades and Picks Rising.—The
National Debt to be Paid
When Custer Returns.

11. Reynolds' Sioux City interview is reported by the Bismarck *Tribune*, Aug. 19, 1874.

The story that Samuel Barrows sent back to New York was more sensible; he cautioned his readers that the miners, though undeniably skilled and truthful, had no way to determine the extent and value of the gold field. He reminded possible adventurers that the region was owned by the Sioux, "who have sworn to repel any intrusion of the white man." And he concluded: "Those who seek the Hills only for gold must be prepared to take their chances. Let the over-confident study the history of Pike's Peak. The Black Hills, too, are not without ready-made monuments for the martyrs who may perish in their parks."[12]

Of all the newsmen the most intemperate was William Eleroy Curtis. After an earlier tentative indication of a gold strike, he filed a dispatch that sent his editors back in Chicago into a journalistic orgy of tub-thumping. The August 27 issue of the *Inter-Ocean* devoted the entire front page to the discovery. "Gold! The Land of Promise—Stirring News from the Black Hills." Then, after a headline with eleven "decks" or subheads, came Curtis' story dated August 7:

> They call it a ten dollar diggin's, and all the camp is aglow with the gold fever. In previous dispatches and letters I have told of the discovery, but the place then hadn't reached the dignified name of "diggin's," and only a few little yellow particles had been washed out of a panful of sand. This is the first opportunity our miners have had to make a really fair test of the "color," and it has yielded them abundantly. . . . From the grass roots down it was "pay dirt," and after a dozen pans or more had been washed out, the two persevering men who will be the pioneers of a new golden State came into camp with a little yellow dust

12. Barrows' dispatch of Aug. 10 in the New York *Tribune* of Aug. 28, 1874.

wrapped carefully up in the leaf of an old account book.[13]

Curtis then reprinted a claim that had been drawn up by twenty-one members of the expedition and posted inside a hardtack box cover at the site. It was headed "District No. 1, Custer Park Mining Company."

Back in Custer's Gulch the men in the main camp waited eagerly for the General to return from his reconnaissance; they had found the gold and they wanted to go home.

13. *Inter-Ocean,* Aug. 27, 1874.

CHAPTER 5

Home the Hard Way

August 4 to August 30

The country around the Cheyenne River was an ugly contrast to the Hills, and Custer was glad to leave it. After sending Reynolds off, he crossed the river with his command in the morning and rode several miles along the lower side, where a few shabby cottonwoods fringed the banks. Beyond the river to the south he could see nothing but desolate plain. Reluctantly, his men filled their canteens with water from the river; it was unpalatable even when first dipped up, and would become actually nauseating when carried for a while, but there would be no other water for twenty miles. As the dry wind rasped their faces, they turned toward the cool highlands and began the march back to the base camp.

When they had reached the Hills again and were nearing camp, Sergeant B. L. Clear came in from a side trip and claimed he had seen a herd of a hundred elk. Apparently some of his colleagues were doubtful, for Professor Donaldson, in relating the incident, felt it necessary to point out that Clear was a truthful and reliable man who had soldiered with Custer for nearly eight years.

At the camp in Custer Park, Colonel Tilford had been in temporary command. One of his first actions on taking over had been to change the time of reveille from 2:45 to 4 A.M. Private Ewert, always suspicious of an officer's motives, said,

"I scarcely think that he done this for the benefit of the men, but simply because he wanted to change existing orders." When Custer returned on August 5 and resumed command, reveille time went back to 2:45 and the men got ready to break camp in the morning and start for home.

After dark, Custer gave One Stab his pony and rifle and a week's rations, and sent him on his way. The worried chief was passed through the picket line quietly so he could put a night's travel between himself and the Arikara scouts. Professor Donaldson reported that the Arikara chief Bear's Ears went to Custer and resigned in disgust after One Stab was released. "Mad Bull (appropriately named) made a great speech, showing that he and Bear's Ears should have been allowed to take out and kill and scalp the poor, old, emaciated, disarmed, unoffending captive. Gentle, magnanimous, noble, christian red men! Heroes and martyrs be they all."[1]

If the troopers expected Custer simply to guide them back over the same old trail, or to take the straightest route home, they were too optimistic. Nothing new could be learned by trudging along the old wagon ruts, watering at the same holes, surmounting the same ridges. Custer meant to see and map as much of the country as he could. The homeward road led north, countermarching along the old trail briefly and then striking out for Bear Butte and the Little Missouri. Perhaps, by sideswiping the backyard of the hostiles, Custer even hoped to provoke Sitting Bull into fighting. The route was practical for the livestock, because once they struck the headwaters of the Heart and turned east there would be plenty of water all the way to Fort Lincoln.

1. Donaldson's dispatch of Aug. 8 in the *Daily Pioneer* of Aug. 25, 1874.

CUSTER'S FIRST GRIZZLY

The expedition followed its old trail for thirty miles or so, then turned eastward across a high prairie in the direction of Bear Butte. Custer was far ahead of his train on August 7 when, after crossing a ridge and locating a fine campsite, he realized a lifetime ambition. His scout Bloody Knife discovered a grizzly bear on the side of a hill, about seventy-five yards away, and Custer fired a shot that struck the animal in the thigh. The bear wheeled, and another shot from Custer's Remington and three more from Ludlow and Bloody Knife put him down. A knife thrust to the jugular by Bloody Knife dispatched him absolutely. He was a very old male with worn and broken teeth and a body riddled with scars.

Dragging the carcass onto a flat rock, the men summoned Illingworth for a photograph. While Custer, Ludlow, Bloody Knife, and an orderly posed behind the body, Illingworth made a view that would soon be on sale in stationery shops throughout the East (Figure 10).

Nobody asked whether or not Custer's bullet had been the fatal one. It was Custer's bear the way it was Custer's expedition.

THE ELK DANCE

On August 8, soon after breaking camp before daylight, the train was enveloped in a great fog that made travel impossible. Fires were built and the men huddled around them until midmorning when the sun broke through. Next day the soldiers killed a hundred deer, mainly white-tailed. The discovery of some grass fires caused Custer to issue a circular ordering the rear guard company henceforth to remain in camp half an hour after the departure of the train, to make sure that all fires were out. Any company that left a dangerous campfire was to become the pioneer corps for the rest of the trip.

The Arikaras killed their first elk August 10, resulting in a celebration described by Professor Donaldson—who was less than appreciative.

> In the evening they had an Elk Feast and Dance. The entertainment was in the edge of the pine forest, and around the bright camp fires. Whole sides of the elk were set up to roast, on long pins stuck in the ground. It was well cooked. They decline salt on their fresh meats. While the meat was roasting, they danced to the music of sticks beat on frying pans and tin wash basins. It was perfect in time, but lacked everything else to charm. We are apt to consider dancing as easy and graceful, lithe and fascinating. But in the Ree's dancing, all these were wanting, and everything else (except time) that could render it pleasing. They never straighten up; but keep the knees bent and the body inclined forward, while the head is thrown up to stare around. Each one dances independently of all the others, except that they jostle against and stumble over one another. They jerk up their feet and stamp them on the ground as awkwardly and as clumsily as bears, clowns, or Calibans. They make no vocal symphonies, but grunt and whoop-howl and groan. Some wore trousers and others leggins and breech cloths. Some wore shirts and others only blankets. They were barefoot, or else wore moccasins, boots or shoes. On their heads were hats, or caps, or cloths, or only long, laughing, black locks. Their clothing was as diverse in color

as in kind. Uneducated pigs or ourangoutangs could excel them.[2]

THE DEATH OF PRIVATE KING

By August 12 the expedition had reached the eastern edge of the Black Hills and was ready to head due north to Bear Butte. Illingworth collected all the officers and scientists in front of the headquarters tent and made a staff photograph (Figure 12) that later would be widely published and mislabeled. It would be published by at least one historian as a product of the Yellowstone expedition of 1873, and many attempts would be made to identify the persons in the picture. One officer would be identified by a twentieth-century writer as Major Marcus Reno, who was not with the expedition.

Private James King of Company H fell ill on August 12, giving Private Ewert another opportunity to rail at his superiors. Ewert wrote that King fainted twice in the sun but was still marked for duty, and when he finally could ride no longer he had to crawl into a wagon because all the ambulances were full of owls, snakes, and Negro servants. King died the following afternoon. He was sewn in a swatch of canvas and ordered to be buried the same evening, but Colonel Tilford declared that no man in his battalion would be buried a mere two hours after death if he could prevent it. He insisted, according to Ewert, that if Custer could not wait with his train in the morning, the left wing would hold back and perform the burial. Custer did not wait, so the left wing stayed in camp August 14 long enough to get Private King's body into the ground. Colonel Benteen read the service, and Ewert wrote: "In the grey twilight of morning,

2. Donaldson's dispatch of Aug. 15 in the *Daily Pioneer* of Aug. 26, 1874.

the men with bowed heads, tears trickling down the sunburnt cheeks, the dead body suspended over the grave, the
Captain with his grey hair reading the service, the silence,
all are impressed on my memory never to be erased."

THE LAST MAIL

Geologists call Bear Butte a laccolith. It is an isolated
granite blister, sent up red-hot from the earth's core and
standing alone, inevitably tempting travelers to call it a lone
sentinel. Rising twelve hundred feet above the prairie floor,
it supports a scant vegetation of red cedar, yellow pine,
lichens, and grass. Donaldson and Winchell climbed it,
using old deer and antelope trails, after the command
pitched camp five miles south of its base on August 14.

In camp, Custer issued a circular announcing that the
mail would go out tomorrow by Indian scout and that each
company would be allowed three ounces. To General Terry
at St. Paul he sent a dispatch asking that a paymaster meet
the command at Fort Lincoln, and to his wife he penned a
final note:

> My darling Sunbeam—I cannot tell you how hard
> and earnestly I have worked to make this expedition a
> success. I have been, not only Commanding Officer,
> but also guide, among other things. We have been in
> and through the Black Hills—and I have the proud
> satisfaction of knowing that our explorations have
> exceeded the most sanguine expectations, but that my
> superior officers will be pleased with the extent and
> thoroughness of these.
>
> The camp Photographer has a complete stereopticon
> view of the Black Hills Country.
>
> I have reached the hunter's highest round of fame.
> . . . I have killed my Grizzly.

We reach Lincoln about the 31st. There has been
no drunkenness, no card-playing on this trip.[3]

ONE MORE INDIAN ALARM

Now they were in open country, soon to be skirting the
headwaters of the Moreau, crossing their old trail in Prospect
Valley, tapping the head of the Grand, then following
roughly the east side of the Little Missouri. Custer sent
around a circular requiring his command to be particularly
alert to possible attack. He forbade herders and stable guards
to pitch shelter tents while on duty, and renewed his orders
regarding the strict use of sidelines and lariats on the
grazing stock. Pickets were to stay on duty until the sound-
ing of the "general" in the mornings. All men absent from
the column without permission were to be arrested.[4]

August 16, when the expedition was in the neighborhood
of the Belle Fourche, four Indians from the Cheyenne
Agency were intercepted by Custer's scouts. They said they
were on the way to the agency from a hostile camp, from
which they had departed only yesterday, and that six bands
of hostiles were waiting along the Little Missouri to attack
the column. It was a tissue of lies. The four fun-loving
wanderers trotted off across the plains after planting their
rumor, while the scouts raced to tell Custer the news.

A thrill of expectation and a mild flurry of belt-tightening
and cartridge-counting ran through the command. Fred
Grant wrote in his journal that a fight was expected soon.

3. Custer to Mrs. Custer, Aug. 15, 1874, in Merington, pp. 274–75.
Compare this version with the one in Mrs. Custer's *Boots and Saddles*,
pp. 294–95. Mrs. Custer seems to have rewritten, and often expanded,
many of her husband's letters before publication. Compare the version
of the General's letter of July 15, 1874, in *Boots and Saddles*, pp. 299–
302, with the same letter in Merington, pp. 272–74.
4. Circular No. 28, Aug. 15, 1874.

But the train rolled on, tense and watchful, and saw not a single hostile Indian.

How the rumor got back to the Missouri River settlements so soon is hard to say. A mail carrier from Fort Rice arrived at Fort Sully about August 20, claiming he had met one of Custer's scouts who told him there had been a great battle. The report was wired to Sheridan, the newspapers picked it up, and soon the whole country was alive with the word that four thousand Indians had jumped Custer along the Little Missouri. The best guess is that while the Arikara mail carriers were leaving the column they picked up the rumor of an impending battle. Encountering the Fort Rice mail rider some days later, they told him what they supposed was true, that a fight actually had occurred.

HELL ON HORSES AND RIDERS

The trip from the Belle Fourche to the Little Missouri was an ordeal for men and livestock. By August 18 Private Ewert was writing that many horses were too weak to carry their riders and were being led bareback. Barrows told of a lame sorrel which, abandoned in a spot where he would have plenty of grass and water, would not give up his place in his company. He limped through an entire day's march and finally had to be shot.

The mules, too, were suffering. Barrows described a worn-out mule as a walking transparency with drooping ears and a disconsolate tail, "a parody on Gothic architecture." On August 19, after a tremendous march of 35.5 miles without water, the pack of broken, crippled animals had grown much larger and four horses were shot.

Something or someone had fired the prairie.

As far as the eye could see, the grass had been burned away. It was natural for the men to suppose that hostile

Indians were seeking to embarrass the expedition; but the
fifty to seventy-five miles of blackened earth could have
been created by a campfire spark, a stroke of lightning, or
other natural causes. There was one advantage: the flames
that ate the grass also consumed the damnable cacti and
made marching easier. Somehow Custer always found
enough grass to keep his livestock going, though it meant
some long and grueling days.

At last, a kind of oasis was reached. They descended into
the valley of the Little Missouri and found wood, water, and
plenty of dry grass. "It was astonishing," said ambulance
driver Fred Snow, "to see Horses and Mules that could
scarcely move during the day—Trot and even run to the
water. The stream was literally black with them. It was very
shallow and many of them laid down and could not rise
without assistance."

Remaining in camp August 20 to rest the men and livestock, Custer could look back on a period of five days in
which he had averaged thirty miles of marching. The worst
was behind him; he would follow the Heart on in, with
grass and water aplenty.

Discipline began to lag as the end of the journey neared,
and one of the offenders was Custer's old antagonist, Colonel
Tilford. The colonel lost his wagon by breaking a standing
order. This note brought him the news:

Headqr's Black Hills Expedition
August 25th 1874

Col. Tilford
The General directs that you at once turn over your
wagon to the Qrmster as it was hauling water for K & H
Companies.
He also directs me to say that he considers your
allowing your wagon to carry Water Kegs a direct

violation of existing orders on your part and the part
of the two Company Commanders.

> Respectfully
> James Calhoun
> 1st Lieut 7th Cavalry
> A.A.A. General[5]

According to Private Ewert, Custer also permitted his
quartermaster, Algernon Smith, to tie a teamster to a wagon
wheel for several hours because the man had let two of his
mules loose to stray among the tents in camp.

Those exhausting marches had filled the sick report.
There were invalids in every company, and one very sick
man indeed. Sergeant Charles Sempker of Company L died
of "chronic diarrhea" and was buried on the evening of
August 26 with his own company in attendance. The obit-
uary expert, Professor Donaldson, penned another cliché.
"The good man and the faithful officer calmly and peace-
fully sleeps alone, to be wakened only by the reveille which
shall call into one general assembly the dead of all the
earth."[6]

On the last day of the march, August 30, the infantry
boys chattered, sang, and bounced along as if they could
walk forever. The wagons, mostly empty, rolled behind the
swinging mule tails at a pace that would have seemed killing
on the outward leg of the journey. The band played. The
scouts and flankers hung close in, to be near the excited
troopers.

They were not due at Fort Lincoln until the following day,
but since they had begun marching at 3 A.M., and by noon
had reached the Heart River crossing twelve miles above

5. Custer's order and dispatch book, p. 46.
6. Donaldson's dispatch of Aug. 30 in the *Daily Pioneer* of Sept. 3,
1874.

the fort, Custer decided to take a long noon and then go in. Colonel Verling Hart had ridden ahead the day before when two scouts had brought him word from Fort Rice that his child was dying. Now Custer, determined that nobody else should leave and spread word of the triumphant arrival, threw a picket line out in front of the column.

Once during the day, probably at the noontime halt, William Illingworth set up his camera and photographed the entire command (Figure 11). Then with a happy shout the teamsters whipped the mules against the traces for the last time, to end an assignment that had taken them 883 miles. Adding the separate side trips made on horseback, the expedition had surveyed 1,205 miles.

Proud of all this newly made history, the men of the Seventh traveled the last mile with faces beaming. Out in front were Lieutenant Wallace's scouts, dressed in new calico shirts presented by the sutler. Behind them came the mounted officers, drawn up in a single line with Custer at the center. The band came next, then the trumpeters, then the cavalry companies in columns of four. The wagon train followed and the infantrymen trailed behind, as usual.

A sentry at Fort Lincoln saw the column coming and spread the word. From stables and barracks, soldiers poured forth to welcome the regiment. Every dwelling, from the officers' houses on the hill to the Indian lodges down along the river, yielded up women and children. The Indian women began to chant, but their thin voices were covered by the brassy clamor of the band playing "Garry Owen," the famed battle quickstep of the Seventh. As the column passed the officers' quarters, each officer dropped out of line to embrace his wife and retire toward his home. Mrs. Custer stepped forward to meet the General and fainted in his arms. ("A very pretty piece of by-play for the men of the

Command," grumbled Private Ewert.) She recovered in a moment.

An orderly led his horse away, and the General was home once more. The shrewd trailmaker, the boisterous jokester, the eager collector of horned toads and petrified wood, the untiring engine that had driven an expedition to El Dorado, was back again. He could not know that within two years men would be repeating a sad little platitude, saying that the miners who had shoveled the gold out of the ground, back there in the evergreen valley, had dug the grave of George Armstrong Custer.

CHAPTER 6

The Course of Empire

August 31 and beyond

The little river towns from Bismarck to Omaha were seeth-
ing with excitement and wonder. Custer had made a
landfall in paradise, given the economy a lift, brought a
glint to the eye of the railroad financier, the merchant, the
land speculator, the idle laborer, the languishing adventurer.

By the time the expedition had disbanded and the news of
gold had saturated the nation, half the men in Bismarck
(said the local *Tribune*) were planning to go prospecting.
Undoubtedly the other half were planning to sell the pros-
pectors wagons, forage, food, and mining equipment. Bismarck immediately implied through the columns of the
Tribune and the dispatches that went out to the Eastern
papers that only a fool would consider routing himself
through any other town. The diagonal line from Bismarck to
Bear Butte was closer and safer than any other route. If
you went through Yankton you would need to cross the
Sioux reservation and pass near some large agencies. If you
tried it from Columbus, Nebraska, you would encounter
desert between the heads of the Loup and the Niobrara with
no wood and little water—not to mention the risk of crossing
the Pawnee reservation. Coming up from Fort Laramie was
no better, the Bismarck promoters insisted, because the
route ran through Red Cloud and Spotted Tail country.[1]

1. Bismarck *Tribune*, Oct. 14, 1874.

Sioux City and Yankton fought back undismayed. It was closer to the Black Hills from Chicago via their route than via Bismarck, and better outfits were available in their towns. "Summing up," cried the Yankton *Press and Dakotaian*, "those intending to visit the Black Hills must inevitably be led to the conclusion that the best, cheapest, most expeditious, and only feasible route to the Black Hills, is via Sioux City, over the Dakota Southern Railroad to Yankton; and from Brule City, D.T., up White Earth River to Harney's Peak. From Yankton westward, the fast and elegant steamers run up the Missouri river through a country of the most picturesque, varied and romantic scenery."[2]

On the night of August 29, even before the expedition had returned, a meeting was held at the St. Charles Hotel in Yankton. It was the same old crowd that had vowed to breach the Hills back in the sixties, plus many a new face. Senator W. W. Brookings sounded the keynote:

"We must congratulate ourselves on the splendid prospect for all southern Dakota. Every farmer or dealer must receive more for his articles sold; a score of hotels would be full; in short, Yankton's rapidly increasing business must be doubled in the next year, to meet the demands of this new El Dorado. That country [the Black Hills] must be opened at once, doubling or quadrupling our already large immigration."

Brookings advised every farmer between the Big Sioux and the Missouri to cut and stack all the hay possible. Miners leaving for the Hills next spring, before grass came, would be willing to pay $5.00 a ton for it.

The group chose a name, the Yankton and Black Hills Mining and Agricultural Company, and took steps to encourage the government to open the Hills. Senator Brookings reminded the audience that their interests coin-

2. Yankton *Press and Dakotaian*, Aug. 27, 1874.

cided with those of the railroads, and advised them to com-
bine their efforts with the Illinois Central and the Dakota
Southern.[3]

During these first post-expedition days, the unknown
factor was the stand to be taken by the government. The
sane view was an obvious one: the Black Hills belonged
exclusively to the Sioux Indians. Every miner who could
read was reminded daily of this, for the papers were full
of discussion. A reporter interviewed General Forsyth in
Chicago:

"Are there many ways to get to it?"

"There are several. The best way, I think, would be to go
through the Red Cloud agency. But you cannot go."

"It is said a good many have started."

"It is a mistake. It would be impossible for any party to
get there now, except a strong military force. No party of
emigrants, armed as they generally are, could do it."[4]

Everyone hoped the government had a plan of action.
Men like Oliver Shannon, in Yankton, insisted that Washington "would never be guilty of the absurdity of sending
Custer's army to explore the mineral wealth of this territory,
and then shut it up for the Sioux who will not enter or
mine there."[5]

This classified advertistment ran in the *Press and Dakotaian,* September 3:

> No sensible man will think of going to the Black Hills
> without first insuring his life. The Missouri Valley Life
> Insurance Co. of Leavenworth, Kan. offers peculiar
> advantages to such. For further particulars apply to
> Nathan Ford, Manager for Dakota.

3. Ibid., Sept. 3, 1874.
4. Chicago *Tribune,* Sept. 4, 1874.
5. *Press and Dakotaian,* Sept. 3, 1874.

No sensible man, in fact, could expect the military and civilian officials of Washington to let him openly enter the Hills in violation of the 1868 treaty. Verification of this came soon, with a letter from Acting Secretary of the Interior B. R. Cowan to Dakota's territorial governor, J. L. Pennington. Secretary Cowan said the question of opening up the Black Hills to settlement rested with Congress, "and until action has been taken by that body this department has no discretion in the matter, but is required and will endeavor to prevent any violation of any provisions of the treaty. . . . All applications for permission to visit the Black Hills country will be denied."[6]

Secretary Cowan reminded Governor Pennington of what the West had conveniently forgotten: the expedition had been primarily a military reconnaissance, not a gold-digging adventure. The military men were still very much in the picture, for it now appeared that armed force would be required to keep miners out of the Hills. This telegram passed from Sheridan to Terry:

> Should the companies now organizing at Sioux City and Yankton trespass on the Sioux Indian Reservation, you are hereby directed to use the force at your command to burn the wagon trains, destroy the outfits and arrest the leaders, confining them at the nearest military post in the Indian country. Should they succeed in reaching the interior you are directed to send such force of cavalry in pursuit as will accomplish the purpose above named. Should Congress open up the country for settlement by extinguishing the treaty rights of the Indians, the undersigned will give a cordial support to the settlement of the Black Hills.[7]

6. Cowan to Pennington, Sept. 8, in *Press and Dakotaian*, Sept. 10, 1874.

7. Telegram of Sept. 3 in *Press and Dakotaian*, Sept. 10, 1874.

Some Yankton citizens responded to this directive by organizing a group called the Black Hills Pioneers. They passed a resolution condemning Sheridan's stand, calling it a usurpation of authority, and they resolved to go ahead with plans for an exploration, "taking all reasonable precaution against the possibility of a collision with the military authorities."

PROFESSOR WINCHELL'S BOMBSHELL

Soon after Newton H. Winchell returned to the University of Minnesota, he was invited to appear before the Academy of Natural Sciences in Minneapolis and discuss the geology of the Black Hills. During his lecture he said that he personally had seen no gold, and no one had brought him a sample of genuine gold to identify during his stay in the Hills. He voiced doubt that any gold was present and he questioned the character of the miners who, he believed, had "talked up" the expedition and persuaded the Army to undertake it.

The reaction was immediate and vigorous. The New York papers carried an account of his lecture[8] and believed what he said. The Western papers quoted him and reviled him. Said the Bismarck *Tribune:* "If Professor Winchell has made such reports . . . he has written himself an ass, and deserves the appelation of a Dogberry of the first water."[9] The newspaper then ticked off the names of others who had seen with their own eyes the gold of Custer's Gulch: Colonel Tilford, John W. Smith, a number of teamsters—and, of course, Custer himself.

Members of the expedition recalled that Winchell had been climbing Harney's Peak on August 1 when much of

8. See New York *Times,* Sept. 14, 1874, p. 2.
9. Bismarck *Tribune,* Sept. 16, 1874.

the gold was found, and had left the next day on a scout to the south. During his absence, more gold had been panned. And besides, asked the editor of the Bismarck paper, when did a geologist ever discover a single gold mine in all recorded history?

Some months later Custer would declare, "Why Professor Winchell saw no gold was simply due to the fact that he neglected to look for it."[10] The General was allowing himself to be quoted amply on the side of the promoters. The Indians did not occupy the Hills, were not miners, and ought to be made to give up the region for the good of white civilization.

A college professor could be written off as addlepated and absentminded, and his opinion could be discounted in the face of so much testimony on the other side. But then Fred Grant, back in Washington, began to grumble that he had not really seen any gold either. Here was a different sort of chap altogether—a friend of Custer's, a hearty drinker, an easygoing young fellow that everyone liked, and the son of a President besides—and *he* had seen no gold.

The Bismarck editor met the problem by assuming that Grant had been misquoted. It was generally believed, at first, that "young Fred would never say such a thing." But he certainly had said it, and accused the miners of chicanery, in his journal:

> We had several Miners along who had nothing to lose and everything to gain; they all lived together and could concoct any plan they wished. After we got near Harney's Peak they said they found gold. Now the country in that region is full of Mica Schist and a very coarse feldsparthic granite. I have been in and around

10. Custer's letter of Dec. 13, 1874, to the New York *World*, reprinted in the *Army and Navy Journal*, Jan. 9, 1875.

a great many gold and silver mines in my life and have never seen this class of stone on mining grounds. Also they came each day and showed specimens and would say "I got this from one pan of earth to-day" and I noticed that they showed the same pieces every day. Then they told about what could be produced saying that one man could get from 10 to 100 dollars a day. I saw about all the gold that was produced in the hands of the different miners, and I don't believe there was two dollars all put together and that they took out there with them. I washed for gold once myself and could not get a color. . . . I don't believe that any gold was found at all.[11]

On the basis of Fred Grant's statements to the newspapers, and some official releases from Washington, the Eastern press began to assume that the alleged gold strike, if not a hoax, was at least a clumsy error. The New York *Times* observed dryly that the information it received from the West about the gold was always accompanied by glowing praise of Bismarck and the Northern Pacific Railroad. An Associated Press dispatch from Washington declared flatly that no gold had been found.

But in the towns along the Missouri there was no loss of confidence. Bitter over the refusal of the military to permit entry into the Hills, the influential men of the river towns advocated flouting the order. One such advocate was the editor of the Bismarck *Tribune*, who wrote a blueprint for lawbreaking. Two hours would put an expedition beyond the military lines, he said, beyond the reach of the telegraph. An expedition of one hundred men could be put across the

11. Fred Grant's journal is in Grant to Acting Adjutant General, Division of the Missouri, Sept. 7, 1874, LR, Division of the Missouri, No. 4385 (1874), RG 98, NA.

river at half a dozen different points without being observed; and once across, a few hours of marching would take them to one of Custer's trails to the Hills. "Of course the military must be avoided, and whatever movements are made must be made quickly and secretly; no party should start with the avowed intention of going to the Black Hills."[12]

It is difficult to avoid a suspicion that to some men on the frontier, the truth of the gold reports was not important; the important thing was the popular belief that the gold was there. A rush of hopeful miners to the frontier would stimulate trade, strengthen the position of the territories, and force a showdown with the Indians.

THE GORDON PARTY

The first group to reach the Hills left Sioux City in October, headed originally by Thomas H. Russell but later by John Gordon and Eph Witcher. Among the twenty-eight adventurers was Mrs. Annie D. Tallent, who was to win fame as the first American woman in the Black Hills (skin color being a technicality that kept Sarah Campbell, the Negro cook with Custer's sutler, from holding the title). The Gordon party posed as a common immigrant group bound for the O'Neill settlement in Nebraska, but it soon crossed the Niobrara and entered the Sioux reservation, then pushed on to French Creek. These pioneers suffered much from cold and privation, and one member died, but they managed to survive the winter and build a stockade and a few cabins. Then they were forced by the Army to leave the Hills.[13]

12. Sept. 9, 1874.

13. For the Gordon episode, see Kingsbury, 1:893–95, and Annie D. Tallent, *The Black Hills; Or, The Last Hunting Ground of the Dakotahs* (Chicago, 1885).

During the winter of 1874–75 the Army tried hard to carry out its orders and enforce the Sioux treaty. The futility of the operation may be seen in this dispatch from a correspondent for the New York *Tribune:*

> The day after Christmas, when all of us were keeping our holidays as merrily as we could, General Guy V. Henry marched out of Fort Laramie with a company of as gallant cavalrymen as ever went to battle, under orders from Washington to find and disperse the miners in the Black Hills!—as senseless an order as if he had been commanded to find a dozen roc's eggs in Sinbad's valley. They went without questioning, into a danger as real and more gratuitous than that of Balaklava, and wandered for days, which must have seemed like years, through the trackless wastes of the Mauvaises Terres, in the execution of impossible orders; and at last the maimed and frozen remnants of the brave company came out at Red Cloud Agency, not a miner having been seen, but their duty performed![14]

By spring the western military units were thoroughly sick of their assignment. It was so plainly impossible to keep the miners out, and so plainly contrary to the will of the people, that vigilance waned. "It's the same old story," General William T. Sherman said in St. Louis, "the story of Adam and Eve and the forbidden fruit." Sherman conceded that there might be some gold in the Black Hills, but he thought it was sparse. "A man might dig sixteen dollars a day, but his meals cost him three dollars apiece, or nine dollars a day, and everything else in proportion . . . and though there may be, as I have no doubt there is, gold in those hills, it is

14. Quoted in *Army and Navy Journal*, May 1, 1875.

comparatively inaccessible from the expense attendant upon digging it out."[15]

So ran one more opinion on the matter of gold. There was so much conflicting testimony about a question which had now assumed national importance that there seemed but one logical move for the government to make. It needed to send in another expedition, with a full-fledged scientific team. With the findings of engineers, geologists, and miners at their disposal, President Grant and his advisers could at last decide what was to be done about the Sioux occupation of the region.

THE JENNEY EXPEDITION

The first man to say in print that another expedition might be needed was William Eleroy Curtis, who said it in Custer's Gulch when the gold strike was very young. In his dispatch of August 3 to the New York *World,* he suggested that a longer visit to the Hills, with many practical miners to prospect the region carefully, ought to be undertaken the next spring.[16]

When spring came and a second expedition was decided upon, Washington's first impulse was to put Custer in charge of it. The news went out. James Gordon Bennett of the New York *Herald* immediately sent Custer an invitation to keep his newspaper ahead on all matters connected with the expedition. Bennett invited Custer to write stories, signed or unsigned, and gave the General a code word, "alta," to send if he consented.[17]

15. St. Louis *Globe,* quoted in *Army and Navy Journal,* May 1, 1875.
16. In the *World,* Aug. 16, 1874.
17. Bennett's letter of April 1, 1875, in package 31, E. B. Custer Collection, Custer Battlefield National Monument, Crow Agency, Montana.

Then the government decided that Custer's presence would automatically make the expedition a military one in the minds of the Indians. Better to put it under the direction of the Department of Interior, it was thought, and put a lesser known commander in charge of the escort.

Early in May, 1875, Colonel Richard I. Dodge's six cavalry and two infantry companies took a scientific team into the Hills by way of Fort Laramie. Leader of the civilians was Walter P. Jenney, of the New York School of Mines. His early reports from Castle Creek and French Creek were so discouraging that many people thought he was purposely understating the situation. Later his language grew more hopeful. He moved north into regions not covered by Custer, and diligently sank holes by the score whenever he sensed that gold might be present. His final conclusions were conservative but favorable. He saw little hope that individual miners, working with primitive pan and rocker, could succeed; but he felt that teams of miners with more sophisticated equipment could bring out gold in profitable amounts.[18]

The Hills were teeming now with miners, many of whom helped Jenney with his prospecting. He estimated there were about eight hundred white men in the area. Because the government had already begun negotiations with the Indians to purchase the gold fields, and the presence of these intruders was embarrassing to the treaty-makers, the Army made one more attempt to clear them out. Late in July 1875, General George Crook called a meeting of the trespassers at his camp near Harney's Peak and read an ultimatum. Crook handled the touchy situation well and avoided antagonizing the miners. His proclamation of July 29 suggested "that the miners now in the hills assemble at the

18. See Walter P. Jenney, *Report on the Mineral Wealth, Climate and Rainfall and Natural Resources of the Black Hills of Dakota,* 44th Cong., 1 Sess., Exec. Doc. No. 51.

military post about to be established at Camp Harney, near the stockade on French Creek [Gordon's old stockade], on or about the 10th day of August; that they then and there hold a meeting and take such steps as may seem best to them by organization and the drafting of proper resolutions to secure to each, when the country shall have been opened, the benefit of his discovery and the labor he has already expended."

The miners were so pleased with the promise of a clear field later, and so impressed by Crook's forthrightness, that they drew up a proclamation of their own to thank him for "the kind and gentlemanly manner with which his command have executed his [the President's] order."[19]

For some, the first glow was wearing off the New El Dorado. Clearly there were no nuggets in the grass roots, and getting the gold was not going to be easy. Back in the East the I-told-you-so period was beginning. "Of the great army of adventurers who marched hopefully across the Nebraska sand drives in search of gold," said the Chicago *Times*, "not one, so far, has brought back a hundred dollars in gold." The newspaper quoted the superintendent of a Chicago smelting works as saying he had made more than twenty assays of gold quartz from the Black Hills, and not one specimen had possessed a value of $75 per ton.[20]

The future of the Hills, though, was certain. There was going to be a boom. There was going to be a town called Custer, and one called Deadwood, and one quaint sidehill town called Lead where the big Homestake mine would grow; there would be stagecoach routes and dance halls and gunfights, and all the goings-on that later generations could transmute into legend. Wild Bill Hickok, Calamity Jane,

19. *Army and Navy Journal,* Oct. 16, 1875.
20. Quoted in ibid.

Jack McCall, all surely coming—but one ponderous obstacle stood in the way: the Black Hills were the property of the Teton Sioux.

THE TREATY COMMISSION

In the spring of 1875, government officials invited Red Cloud, Spotted Tail, and other chiefs to Washington for a council. Red Cloud was quarreling at the time with his agent, Dr. J. J. Saville, and arrived at the Capitol filled with complaints about the mishandling of his agency. Believing that he had been called to air his grievances, he was startled to find Spotted Tail and the others on hand. They all sensed that big medicine was about to be made. When the subject of the Black Hills came up, the chiefs bristled, listened to the harangues of the whites, and answered that they could do no bargaining until they had consulted their people. Their disgruntled sponsors put them on the next train for the West, promising that in the fall a special commission would come out to meet the whole Sioux nation and discuss the purchase of the Hills.

An Iowa senator, William B. Allison, headed the commission; serving with him were General Alfred Terry, the Reverend S. D. Hinman (missionary to the Santees), and seven others. They were instructed to represent the interests of the Indians as well as the whites, and they did their best, but they were engaged in a kind of musical comedy plot which could only make them look ridiculous in the eyes of most Westerners. They met the Indians, twenty thousand of them, on the White River eight miles east of the Red Cloud Agency.

The young men of the assembled Teton bands were angry and full of steam, and had no desire to sell the Black Hills at any price. The nonfighters, including the old men, the cripples, the women, the peaceable drones, and the dawdlers, wanted to sell but had listened to some bad advice. Friendly white men, some well-meaning and others venal, had assured the Indians that the Hills were worth hundreds of millions of dollars. The commission had neither the authority nor the inclination to pay a fabulous price.

There was some preliminary horseplay, not all of it funny. Crowds of young mounted braves swarmed about the commissioners, shouting *Hoka hey,* the call for a charge; then the parley moved into the elocutionary stage. The Indians presented their demands:

RED DOG: We want to be taken care of for seven generations ahead.

RED CLOUD: There have been six nations raised, and I am the seventh, and I want seven generations to be fed.

LITTLE BEAR: Our Great Father has a house full of money. Suppose a man walks right into that house and takes the money, do you suppose that would suit everybody? The Black Hills are the house of gold for the Indians. We watch it to get rich. For the last four years the Great Father's men are working at that hill, and I want our Great Father to remember that and not to forget it.

SPOTTED TAIL: As long as we live on this earth we will expect pay. We want to leave the amount with the President at interest forever. By doing that I think it will be so that I can live. I want to live on the interest of my money. . . . Part of this each year I can trade for something to eat. I will trade part of it for enough annuity-goods to go around. I will trade some of it for stock to raise cattle. I will trade some of it for hogs.

When Spotted Tail asked the commissioners to put their offer in writing, Senator Allison proposed to pay $400,000 a year for the mining rights, or to buy the Hills outright for $6,000,000. The Indians declined the offer and on September 29 the conference ended in failure.

When the commissioners submitted their report, they admitted that no course of action seemed open except a strong stand by Congress. They recommended that Congress fix a fair evaluation for the Black Hills and insist that the Indians accept the offer. And what club could be held over the heads of the chiefs? Simply the fact that the issuance of rations provided in the treaty of 1868 was for four years only; that period had long expired and the government was feeding the Indians out of a sense of humanity. It could starve them into submission whenever it chose. If the chiefs failed to sell the Black Hills, their women and children might suffer.[21]

BUGLES IN THE AFTERNOON

It was all over now, and the chiefs knew it. The agency chiefs were growing docile, but not those hardheads along the Yellowstone and the Powder—Crazy Horse, Sitting Bull, Gall, and the others. Joined daily by more fearful or truculent malcontents from the agencies, and swollen by enlistees from the Northern Cheyennes, the ranks of the hostiles were growing large and the patience of the U.S. Army was waning.

No story in American history falls more easily from the

21. My account of the purchase of the Black Hills draws heavily on the *Annual Report of the Commissioner of Indian Affairs* for 1875 and 1876. The quotations are from the proceedings of the Sioux Commission in the 1875 report. See also George E. Hyde, *Red Cloud's Folk* (Norman, Okla., 1937), pp. 230–48, for an account with details not contained in the official reports.

lips of schoolboys than the tale of the Little Big Horn. In the winter of 1875–76 the Army, suddenly and rather unaccountably, decided to call every Indian back to his agency without delay. The winter was fierce that year, and the time limit set for the return of the Indians was short. Many families normally living on the reservation were out hunting in the hostile country. Perhaps they got the word, perhaps not. Perhaps they could have returned with their women and children, despite the cruel weather, if they had wanted to. But they did not come in. Their failure to return branded them as belligerents, and the Army decreed an early campaign against them.

All that is important about that campaign can be told in a single sentence. On a day in June, where the Little Big Horn flows narrow and shallow in the Montana hills, the happy boy general, George Armstrong Custer, divided his command and found himself confronted by too many Indians.

After the death of Custer and 269 of his officers and men, the American people were in no mood to bargain with the Teton Sioux. The proposition offered to Red Cloud and other chiefs by a newly appointed set of commissioners was stern but not avowedly punitive. Among other concessions the Indians were to surrender the Black Hills in return for rations, schools, and other aids to civilization. They also were to contemplate a move to Indian Territory.

In the little summaries of Black Hills history that turn up in travel literature and on the backs of road maps, Custer's death on the Little Big Horn is linked directly with his discovery of gold. Like most oversimplifications, this one distorts. Custer invaded the Hills, the story goes, and created a gold rush that drove the hostile Indians out of their beloved country and forced them to make a last desperate stand in Montana.

It is almost true. But when viewed in perspective, with all circumstances considered, the story must be qualified.

Was Custer's expedition to the Black Hills a violation of the treaty of 1868? As originally projected it was not a legal violation. It was a military reconnaissance fully permissible under the treaty terms. But the eagerness of the West for gold, and the eagerness of Custer for the limelight, turned it into a great public spectacle. It was Custer who took the miners along; who sent Charley Reynolds on his hazardous sprint down to Fort Laramie with news of the gold strike; who publicly announced upon his return that the Black Hills ought to be taken over by white men. As carried out by Custer, the expedition was a treaty violation in spirit if not in fact.

But Custer's flamboyance only hurried the invasion. The American people had put the Hills on their list many years before, neatly ticketing it as land the Indians did not need. Half a century earlier, more or less, Illinois had been on that same list. And before that, Ohio.

The Indians who jumped Custer in 1876 were not brooding because they were losing the Black Hills, but because they had lost, in their own generation, everything. Perhaps the Hills represented the last bit of proof that nothing would avail against the pressure of white civilization.

When the Indians killed Custer they had not yet lost the Hills, though the loss was imminent. They still were bargaining and not doing badly. They had stood off the Allison treaty commission, and even frightened some of the commissioners with a show of belligerence, and might have received a better price from the government except for the tragedy on the Little Big Horn.

The Indians did not attack Custer because they were angry over the loss of their lands, but because *he* was riding hell-

bent to attack *them*. Custer did not die because he found gold
in the Hills, but because he trapped himself by a foolish
military move. And if there is a villain in the story it is not
peevish old Sitting Bull, or the yellow-haired boy general,
but the American people and their never-ending list of places
which the Indians "did not need."

Appendixes

Appendix 1

SUMMARY OF LOCATIONS AND DISTANCES
(Abstracted from Ludlow, *Report of a Reconnaissance*, p. 121)

DATE	LOCATION	LATITUDE			LONGITUDE			DAY'S MARCH	TOTAL DISTANCE
1874		°	′	″	°	′	″	Miles	Miles
July 2	Buck Creek	46	40	50	101	03	08	15.1	15.1
3		46	35	25	101	08	43	14.1	29.2
4	Dog's Teeth Creek							14.7	43.9
5	Creek Where Bear Winters							16.9	60.8
6	Cannonball River	46	19	52	101	47	43	12.9	73.7
7	Cedar Creek	46	03	20	102	06	07	30.4	104.1
8	Hiddenwood Creek	45	57	20	102	25	01	19.0	123.1
9	Grand River	45	54	58	102	45	43	20.0	143.1
10	Grand River	45	58	00	103	01	42	24.0	167.1
11	Cave	45	49	10	103	26	46	19.7	186.8
12		45	43	20	103	29	10	11.0	197.8
13	Sage Brush Camp	45	35	50	103	38	05	15.5	213.3
14, 15	Prospect Valley	45	28	56	103	47	25	13.0	226.3
16	Border Camp							30.0	256.8
17	Bad Lands	44	58	10	104	02	39	17.7	274.5
18, 19	Belle Fourche	44	48	05	104	08	57	17.5	292.0
20		44	38	35	104	15	27	18.3	310.3
21	Redwater Valley	44	30	18	104	15	52	14.3	324.6
22, 23	Inyan Kara Camp	44	13	00	104	15	57	22.2	346.8
24	Floral Valley	44	12	40	104	11	30	11.0	357.8
25	Floral Valley	44	08	35	104	03	34	11.5	369.3
26, 27	Castle Valley	44	01	45	103	51	20	14.0	383.3
28	Indian Camp	44	00	52	103	48	27	10.0	393.3
29								15.0	408.5
30, 31								10.2	418.7

Appendix I (*continued*)

DATE	LOCATION	LATITUDE	LONGITUDE	DAY'S MARCH	TOTAL DISTANCE
1874		° ′ ″	° ′ ″	Miles	Miles
Aug. 1–5	Permanent Camp	43 46 10	103 33 02	3.5	422.2
6				23.2	445.4
7		44 08 53	103 45 50	16.2	461.6
8		44 15 10	103 38 08	14.7	476.3
9				7.5	483.8
10, 11		44 09 53	103 30 16	7.5	491.3
12		44 07 35	103 26 04	5.7	497.0
13		44 07 46	103 23 48	4.7	501.7
14, 15	Bear Butte Camp	44 23 43	103 25 19	26.0	527.7
16		44 47 35	103 28 02	29.5	557.2
17		45 09 30	103 37 45	28.2	585.4
18	Prospect Valley	45 31 05	103 52 35	30.2	615.6
19				35.3	650.9
20, 21	Little Missouri River	46 08 30	103 51 30	29.9	680.8
22		46 27 20	103 42 54	28.5	709.3
23	Little Missouri River	46 34 55	103 29 25	19.0	728.3
24	Heart River	46 44 45	103 07 51	24.7	753.0
25				17.7	770.7
26	Young Men's Buttes	46 52 20	102 15 49	32.2	802.9
27				17.1	820.0
28	Little Muddy Creek			16.0	836.0
29	White Fish Creek	46 52 00	101 16 18	20.0	856.0
30	Fort Abraham Lincoln	46 46 10	100 50 57	27.3	883.3

Appendix 2

TREATY OF APRIL 29, 1868
(From *U.S. Statutes at Large, 15, 635–40*)

Articles of a treaty made and concluded by and between Lieu-
tenant-General William T. Sherman, General William S.
Harney, General Alfred H. Terry, General C. C. Augur, J. B.
Henderson, Nathaniel G. Taylor, John B. Sanborn, and Samuel F.
Tappan, duly appointed commissioners on the part of the United
States, and the different bands of the Sioux Nation of Indians,
by their chiefs and headmen, whose names are hereto subscribed,
they being duly authorized to act in the premises.

ARTICLE I. From this day forward all war between the
parties to this agreement shall forever cease. The government
of the United States desires peace, and its honor is hereby
pledged to keep it. The Indians desire peace, and they now
pledge their honor to maintain it.

If bad men among the whites, or among other people subject
to the authority of the United States, shall commit any wrong
upon the person or property of the Indians, the United States
will, upon proof made to the agent and forwarded to the Commissioner of Indian Affairs at Washington city, proceed at once
to cause the offender to be arrested and punished according to
the laws of the United States, and also reimburse the injured
person for the loss sustained.

If bad men among the Indians shall commit a wrong or
depredation upon the person or property of any one, white,
black, or Indian, subject to the authority of the United States,
and at peace therewith, the Indians herein named solemnly
agree that they will, upon proof made to their agent and notice
by him, deliver up the wrong-doer to the United States, to be
tried and punished according to its laws; and in case they
wilfully refuse so to do, the person injured shall be reimbursed
for his loss from the annuities or other moneys due or to become
due to them under this or other treaties made with the United

States. And the President, on advising with the Commissioner of Indian Affairs, shall prescribe such rules and regulations for ascertaining damages under the provisions of this article as in his judgment may be proper. But no one sustaining loss while violating the provisions of this treaty or the laws of the United States shall be reimbursed therefor.

ARTICLE II. The United States agrees that the following district of country, to wit, viz: commencing on the east bank of the Missouri river where the forty-sixth parallel of north latitude crosses the same, thence along low-water mark down said east bank to a point opposite where the northern line of the State of Nebraska strikes the river, thence west across said river, and along the northern line of Nebraska to the one hundred and fourth degree of longitude west from Greenwich, thence north on said meridian to a point where the forty-sixth parallel of north latitude intercepts the same, thence due east along said parallel to the place of beginning; and in addition thereto, all existing reservations on the east bank of said river shall be, and the same is, set apart for the absolute and undisturbed use and occupation of the Indians herein named, and for such other friendly tribes or individual Indians as from time to time they may be willing, with the consent of the United States, to admit amongst them; and the United States now solemnly agrees that no persons except those herein designated and authorized so to do, and except such officers, agents, and employés of the government as may be authorized to enter upon Indian reservations in discharge of duties enjoined by law, shall ever be permitted to pass over, settle upon, or reside in the territory described in this article, or in such territory as may be added to this reservation for the use of said Indians, and henceforth they will and do hereby relinquish all claims or right in and to any portion of the United States or Territories, except such as is embraced within the limits aforesaid, and except as hereinafter provided.

ARTICLE III. If it should appear from actual survey or other satisfactory examination of said tract of land that it contains less than one hundred and sixty acres of tillable land for each person who, at the time, may be authorized to reside on it under the provisions of this treaty, and a very considerable number of such persons shall be disposed to commence cultivating the soil as farmers, the United States agrees to set apart, for the use of said Indians, as herein provided, such additional quantity of arable land, adjoining to said reservation, or as near to the same as it can be obtained, as may be required to provide the necessary amount.

ARTICLE IV. The United States agrees, at its own proper expense, to construct at some place on the Missouri river, near the centre of said reservation, where timber and water may be convenient, the following buildings, to wit: a warehouse, a storeroom for the use of the agent in storing goods belonging to the Indians, to cost not less than twenty-five hundred dollars; an agency building for the residence of the agent, to cost not exceeding three thousand dollars; a residence for the physician, to cost not more than three thousand dollars; and five other buildings, for a carpenter, farmer, blacksmith, miller, and engineer, each to cost not exceeding two thousand dollars; also a school-house or mission building, so soon as a sufficient number of children can be induced by the agent to attend school, which shall not cost exceeding five thousand dollars.

The United States agrees further to cause to be erected on said reservation, near the other buildings herein authorized, a good steam circular saw-mill, with a grist-mill and shingle machine attached to the same, to cost not exceeding eight thousand dollars.

ARTICLE V. The United States agrees that the agent for said Indians shall in the future make his home at the agency building; that he shall reside among them, and keep an office open at all times for the purpose of prompt and diligent inquiry into such matters of complaint by and against the Indians as may be presented for investigation under the provisions of their treaty stipulations, as also for the faithful discharge of other duties enjoined on him by law. In all cases of depredation on person or property he shall cause the evidence to be taken in writing and forwarded, together with his findings, to the Commissioner of Indian Affairs, whose decision, subject to the revision of the Secretary of the Interior, shall be binding on the parties to this treaty.

ARTICLE VI. If any individual belonging to said tribes of Indians, or legally incorporating with them, being the head of a family, shall desire to commence farming, he shall have the privilege to select, in the presence and with the assistance of the agent then in charge, a tract of land within said reservation, not exceeding three hundred and twenty acres in extent, which tract when so selected, certified, and recorded in the "land book," as herein directed, shall cease to be held in common, but the same may be occupied and held in the exclusive possession of the person selecting it, and of his family, so long as he or they may continue to cultivate it.

Any person over eighteen years of age, not being the head of a family, may in like manner select and cause to be certified to him or her, for purposes of cultivation, a quantity of land not exceeding eighty acres in extent, and thereupon be entitled to the exclusive possession of the same as above directed.

For each tract of land so selected a certificate, containing a description thereof and the name of the person selecting it, with a certificate endorsed thereon that the same has been recorded, shall be delivered to the party entitled to it, by the agent, after the same shall have been recorded by him in a book to be kept in his office, subject to inspection, which said book shall be known as the "Sioux Land Book."

The President may, at any time, order a survey of the reservation, and, when so surveyed, Congress shall provide for protecting the rights of said settlers in their improvements, and may fix the character of the title held by each. The United States may pass such laws on the subject of alienation and descent of property between the Indians and their descendants as may be thought proper. And it is further stipulated that any male

Indians over eighteen years of age, of any band or tribe that is or shall hereafter become a party to this treaty, who now is or who shall hereafter become a resident or occupant of any reservation or territory not included in the tract of country designated and described in this treaty for the permanent home of the Indians, which is not mineral land, nor reserved by the United States for special purposes other than Indian occupation, and who shall have made improvements thereon of the value of two hundred dollars or more, and continuously occupied the same as a homestead for the term of three years, shall be entitled to receive from the United States a patent for one hundred and sixty acres of land including his said improvements, the same to be in the form of the legal subdivisions of the surveys of the public lands. Upon application in writing, sustained by the proof of two disinterested witnesses, made to the register of the local land office when the land sought to be entered is within a land district, and when the tract sought to be entered is not in any land district, then upon said application and proof being made to the commissioner of the general land office, and the right of such Indian or Indians to enter such tract or tracts of land shall accrue and be perfect from the date of his first improvements thereon, and shall continue as long as he continues his residence and improvements, and no longer. And any Indian or Indians receiving a patent for land under the foregoing provisions, shall thereby and from thenceforth become and be a citizen of the United States, and be entitled to all the privileges and immunities of such citizens, and shall, at the same time, retain all his rights to benefits accruing to Indians under this treaty.

ARTICLE VII. In order to insure the civilization of the Indians entering into this treaty, the necessity of education is admitted, especially of such of them as are or may be settled on said agricultural reservations, and they therefore pledge themselves to compel their children, male and female, between the ages of six and sixteen years, to attend school; and it is hereby made the duty of the agent for said Indians to see that this stipulation is strictly complied with; and the United States agrees that for every thirty children between said ages who can be induced or compelled to attend school, a house shall be provided and a teacher competent to teach the elementary branches of an English education shall be furnished, who will reside among said Indians, and faithfully discharge his or her duties as a teacher. The provisions of this article to continue for not less than twenty years.

ARTICLE VIII. When the head of a family or lodge shall have selected lands and received his certificate as above directed, and the agent shall be satisfied that he intends in good faith to commence cultivating the soil for a living, he shall be entitled to receive seeds and agricultural implements for the first year, not exceeding in value one hundred dollars, and for each succeeding year he shall continue to farm, for a period of three years more, he shall be entitled to receive seeds and implements as aforesaid, not exceeding in value twenty-five dollars.

And it is further stipulated that such persons as commence farming shall receive instruction from the farmer herein provided for, and whenever more than one hundred persons shall enter upon the cultivation of the soil, a second blacksmith shall be provided, with such iron, steel, and other material as may be needed.

ARTICLE IX. At any time after ten years from the making of this treaty, the United States shall have the privilege of withdrawing the physician, farmer, blacksmith, carpenter, engineer, and miller herein provided for, but in case of such withdrawal, an additional sum thereafter of ten thousand dollars per annum shall be devoted to the education of said Indians, and the Commissioner of Indian Affairs shall, upon careful inquiry into their condition, make such rules and regulations for the expenditure of said sum as will best promote the educational and moral improvement of said tribes.

ARTICLE X. In lieu of all sums of money or other annuities provided to be paid to the Indians herein named, under any treaty or treaties heretofore made, the United States agrees to deliver at the agency house on the reservation herein named, on or before the first day of August of each year, for thirty years, the following articles, to wit:

For each male person over fourteen years of age, a suit of good substantial woollen clothing, consisting of coat, pantaloons, flannel shirt, hat, and a pair of home-made socks.

For each female over twelve years of age, a flannel skirt, or the goods necessary to make it, a pair of woollen hose, twelve yards of calico, and twelve yards of cotton domestics.

For the boys and girls under the ages named, such flannel and cotton goods as may be needed to make each a suit as aforesaid, together with a pair of woollen hose for each.

And in order that the Commissioner of Indian Affairs may be able to estimate properly for the articles herein named, it shall be the duty of the agent each year to forward to him a full and exact census of the Indians, on which the estimate from year to year can be based.

And in addition to the clothing herein named, the sum of ten dollars for each person entitled to the beneficial effects of this treaty shall be annually appropriated for a period of thirty years, while such persons roam and hunt, and twenty dollars for each person who engages in farming, to be used by the Secretary of the Interior in the purchase of such articles as from time to time the condition and necessities of the Indians may indicate to be proper. And if within the thirty years, at any time, it shall appear that the amount of money needed for clothing under this article can be appropriated to better uses for the Indians named herein, Congress may, by law, change the appropriation to other purposes; but in no event shall the amount of this appropriation be withdrawn or discontinued for the period named. And the President shall annually detail an officer of the army to be present and attest the delivery of all the goods herein named to the Indians, and he shall inspect and report on the quantity and quality of the goods and the manner of their delivery. And it is hereby expressly stipulated that each Indian over the age of four years, who shall have removed to and settled permanently upon said reservation and complied with the stipulations of this treaty, shall be entitled to receive from the United States, for the period of four years after he shall have settled upon said reservation, one pound of meat and one pound of flour per day, provided the Indians cannot furnish their own subsistence at an earlier date. And it is further stipulated that the United States will furnish and deliver to each lodge of Indians or family of persons legally incorporated with them, who shall remove to the reservation herein described and commence farming, one good American cow, and one good well-broken pair of American oxen within sixty days after such lodge or family shall have so settled upon said reservation.

ARTICLE XI. In consideration of the advantages and benefits conferred by this treaty and the many pledges of friendship by the United States, the tribes who are parties to this agreement hereby stipulate that they will relinquish all right to occupy permanently the territory outside their reservation as herein defined, but yet reserve the right to hunt on any lands north of North Platte, and on the Republican Fork of the Smoky Hill river, so long as the buffalo may range thereon in such numbers as to justify the chase. And they, the said Indians, further expressly agree:

1st. That they will withdraw all opposition to the construction of the railroads now being built on the plains.

2d. That they will permit the peaceful construction of any railroad not passing over their reservation as herein defined.

3d. That they will not attack any persons at home, or travelling, nor molest or disturb any wagon trains, coaches, mules, or cattle belonging to the people of the United States, or to persons friendly therewith.

4th. They will never capture, or carry off from the settlements, white women and children.

5th. They will never kill or scalp white men, nor attempt to do them harm.

6th. They withdraw all pretence of opposition to the construction of the railroad now being built along the Platte river and westward to the Pacific ocean, and they will not in future object to the construction of railroads, wagon roads, mail stations, or other works of utility or necessity, which may be ordered or permitted by the laws of the United States. But should such roads or other works be constructed on the lands of their reservation, the government will pay the tribe whatever amount of damages may be assessed by three disinterested commissioners to be appointed by the President for that purpose, one of said commissioners to be a chief or headman of the tribe.

7th. They agree to withdraw all opposition to the military posts or roads now established south of the North Platte river, or that may be established, not in violation of treaties heretofore made or hereafter to be made with any of the Indian tribes.

ARTICLE XII. No treaty for the cession of any portion or part of the reservation herein described which may be held in common shall be of any validity or force as against the said Indians, unless executed and signed by at least three fourths of all the adult male Indians, occupying or interested in the same; and no cession by the tribe shall be understood or construed in such manner as to deprive, without his consent, any individual member of the tribe of his rights to any tract of land selected by him, as provided in Article VI. of this treaty.

ARTICLE XIII. The United States hereby agrees to furnish annually to the Indians the physician, teachers, carpenter, miller, engineer, farmer, and blacksmiths, as herein contemplated, and that such appropriations shall be made from time to time, on the estimates of the Secretary of the Interior, as will be sufficient to employ such persons.

ARTICLE XIV. It is agreed that the sum of five hundred dollars annually, for three years from date, shall be expended in presents to the ten persons of said tribe who in the judgment of the agent may grow the most valuable crops for the respective year.

ARTICLE XV. The Indians herein named agree that when the agency house and other buildings shall be constructed on the reservation named, they will regard said reservation their permanent home, and they will make no permanent settlement elsewhere; but they shall have the right, subject to the conditions and modifications of this treaty, to hunt, as stipulated in Article XI. hereof.

ARTICLE XVI. The United States hereby agrees and stipulates that the country north of the North Platte river and east of the summits of the Big Horn mountains shall be held and considered to be unceded Indian territory, and also stipulates and agrees that no white person or persons shall be permitted to settle upon or occupy any portion of the same; or without the consent of the Indians, first had and obtained, to pass through the same; and it is further agreed by the United States, that within ninety days after the conclusion of peace with all the bands of the Sioux nation, the military posts now established in the territory in this article named shall be abandoned, and that the road leading to them and by them to the settlements in the Territory of Montana shall be closed.

ARTICLE XVII. It is hereby expressly understood and agreed by and between the respective parties to this treaty that the execution of this treaty and its ratification by the United States Senate shall have the effect, and shall be construed as abrogating and annulling all treaties and agreements heretofore entered into between the respective parties hereto, so far as such treaties and agreements obligate the United States to furnish and provide money, clothing, or other articles of property to such Indians and bands of Indians as become parties to this treaty, but no further.

AGREEMENT OF AUGUST 15, 1876
(From *U.S. Statutes at Large, 19,* 254–57)

Articles of agreement made pursuant to the provisions of an act of Congress entitled "An act making appropriations for the current and contingent expenses of the Indian Department, and for fulfilling treaty stipulations with various Indian tribes, for the year ending June thirtieth, eighteen hundred and seventy seven, and for other purposes," approved August 15, 1876, by and between George W. Manypenny, Henry B. Whipple, Jared W. Daniels, Albert G. Boone, Henry C. Bulis, Newton Edmunds, and Augustine S. Gaylord, commissioners on the part of the United States, and the different bands of the Sioux Nation of Indians, and also the Northern Arapahoes and Cheyennes, by their chiefs and headmen, whose names are hereto subscribed, they being duly authorized to act in the premises.

ARTICLE 1. The said parties hereby agree that the northern and western boundaries of the reservation defined by article 2 of the treaty between the United States and different tribes of Sioux Indians, concluded April 29, 1868, and proclaimed February 24, 1869, shall be as follows: The western boundaries shall commence at the intersection of the one hundred and third meridian of longitude with the northern boundary of the State of Nebraska; thence north along said meridian to its intersection with the South Fork of the Cheyenne River; thence down said stream to its junction with the North Fork; thence up the North Fork of said Cheyenne River to the said one hundred and third meridian; thence north along said meridian to the South Branch of Cannon Ball River or Cedar Creek; and the northern boundary of their said reservation shall follow the said South Branch to its intersection with the main Cannon Ball River, and thence down the said main Cannon Ball River to the Missouri River; and the said Indians do hereby relinquish and cede to the United

States all the territory lying outside the said reservation, as herein modified and described, including all privileges of hunting; and article 16 of said treaty is hereby abrogated.

ARTICLE 2. The said Indians also agree and consent that wagon and other roads, not exceeding three in number, may be constructed and maintained, from convenient and accessible points on the Missouri River, through said reservation, to the country lying immediately west thereof, upon such routes as shall be designated by the President of the United States; and they also consent and agree to the free navigation of the Missouri River.

ARTICLE 3. The said Indians also agree that they will hereafter receive all annuities provided by the said treaty of 1868, and all subsistence and supplies which may be provided for them under the present or any future act of Congress, at such points and places on the said reservation, and in the vicinity of the Missouri River, as the President of the United States shall designate.

ARTICLE 4. The Government of the United States and the said Indians, being mutually desirous that the latter shall be located in a country where they may eventually become self-supporting and acquire the arts of civilized life, it is therefore agreed that the said Indians shall select a delegation of five or more chiefs and principal men from each band, who shall, without delay, visit the Indian Territory under the guidance and protection of suitable persons, to be appointed for that purpose by the Department of the Interior, with a view to selecting therein a permanent home for the said Indians. If such delegation shall make a selection which shall be satisfactory to themselves, the people whom they represent, and to the United States, then the said Indians agree that they will remove to the country so selected within one year from this date. And the said Indians do further agree in all things to submit themselves to such beneficent plans as the Government may provide for them in the selection of a country suitable for a permanent home, where they may live like white men.

ARTICLE 5. In consideration of the foregoing cession of territory and rights, and upon full compliance with each and every obligation assumed by the said Indians, the United States does agree to provide all necessary aid to assist the said Indians in the work of civilization; to furnish to them schools and instruction in mechanical and agricultural arts, as provided for by the treaty of 1868. Also to provide the said Indians with subsistence consisting of a ration for each individual of a pound and a half of beef (or in lieu thereof, one half pound of bacon,) one-half pound of flour, and one-half pound of corn; and for every one hundred rations, four pounds of coffee, eight pounds of sugar, and three pounds of beans, or in lieu of said articles the equivalent thereof, in the discretion of the Commissioner of Indian Affairs. Such rations, or so much thereof as may be necessary, shall be continued until the Indians are able to support themselves. Rations shall, in all cases, be issued to the head of each separate family; and whenever schools shall have been provided by the Government for said Indians, no rations shall be issued for children between the ages of six and fourteen years (the sick and infirm excepted) unless such children shall regularly attend school. Whenever the said Indians shall be located upon lands which are suitable for cultivation, rations shall be issued only to the persons and families of those persons who labor, (the aged, sick, and infirm excepted;) and as an incentive to industrious habits the Commissioner of Indian Affairs may provide that such persons be furnished in payment for their labor such other necessary articles as are requisite for civilized life. The Government will aid said Indians as far as possible in finding a market for their surplus productions, and in finding employment, and will purchase such surplus, as far as may be required, for supplying food to those Indians, parties to this agreement, who are unable to sustain themselves; and will also employ Indians, so far as practicable, in the performance of Government work upon their reservation.

ARTICLE 6. Whenever the head of a family shall, in good faith, select an allotment of land upon such reservation and engage in the cultivation thereof, the Government shall, with his aid, erect a comfortable house on such allotment; and if said Indians shall remove to said Indian Territory as hereinbefore provided, the Government shall erect for each of the principal chiefs a good and comfortable dwelling-house.

ARTICLE 7. To improve the morals and industrious habits of said Indians, it is agreed that the agent, trader, farmer, carpenter, blacksmith, and other artisans employed or permitted to reside within the reservation belonging to the Indians, parties to this agreement, shall be lawfully married and living with their respective families on the reservation; and no person other than an Indian of full blood, whose fitness, morally or otherwise, is not, in the opinion of the Commissioner of Indian Affairs, conducive to the welfare of said Indians, shall receive any benefit from this agreement or former treaties, and may be expelled from the reservation.

ARTICLE 8. The provisions of the said treaty of 1868, except as herein modified, shall continue in full force, and, with the provisions of this agreement, shall apply to any country which may hereafter be occupied by the said Indians as a home; and Congress shall, by appropriate legislation, secure to them an orderly government; they shall be subject to the laws of the United States, and each individual shall be protected in his rights of property, person, and life.

ARTICLE 9. The Indians, parties to this agreement, do hereby solemnly pledge themselves, individually and collectively, to observe each and all of the stipulations herein contained, to select allotments of land as soon as possible after their removal to their permanent home, and to use their best efforts to learn to cultivate the same. And they do solemnly pledge themselves that they will at all times maintain peace with the citizens and Government of the United States; that they will observe the laws thereof and loyally endeavor to fulfill all the obligations assumed by them under the treaty of 1868 and the present agreement, and to this end will, whenever requested by the President of the United States, select so many suitable men from each band to co-operate with him in maintaining order and peace on the reservation as the President may deem necessary, who shall receive such compensation for their services as Congress may provide.

ARTICLE 10. In order that the Government may faithfully fulfill the stipulations contained in this agreement, it is mutually agreed that a census of all Indians affected hereby shall be taken in the month of December of each year, and the names of each head of family and adult person registered; said census to be taken in such manner as the Commissioner of Indian Affairs may provide.

ARTICLE 11. It is understood that the term reservation herein contained shall be held to apply to any country which shall be selected under the authority of the United States as the future home of said Indians.

This agreement shall not be binding upon either party until it shall have received the approval of the President and Congress of the United States.

Appendix 4

ROSTER OF CUSTER'S STAFF
Black Hills Expedition

Commander
  Brevet Major General George A. Custer

Battalion Commanders
  Brevet Brigadier General George A. Forsyth
  Brevet Lieutenant Colonel Joseph G. Tilford

Acting Aide
  Brevet Lieutenant Colonel Frederick Dent Grant

Acting Assistant Adjutant General
  1st Lieutenant James Calhoun

Quartermaster and Commissary
  Brevet Captain Algernon E. Smith

Medical Staff
  Asst. Surgeon J. W. Williams, chief medical officer
  Acting Asst. Surgeon S. J. Allen
  Acting Asst. Surgeon A. C. Bergen

Engineering Detachment
  Brevet Lieutenant Colonel William Ludlow
  W. H. Wood, civilian assistant

Artillery Detachment
  1st Lieutenant Josiah Chance, 17th Infantry

Infantry Battalion
  Company G, 17th Infantry:
                    Brevet Major Louis H. Sanger
                    2nd Lieutenant George H. Roach
  Company I, 20th Infantry:
                    Captain Lloyd Wheaton
                    2nd Lieutenant J. Granville Gates

Indian Scout Detail
    2nd Lieutenant George D. Wallace

Cavalry Officers
    Company A: Captain Myles Moylan
                  2nd Lieutenant Charles Varnum
    Company B: 1st Lieutenant Benjamin Hodgson
                  Brevet Lieutenant Colonel Thomas W. Custer (on special duty commanding Company L)
    Company C: Brevet Lieutenant Colonel Verling K. Hart
                  1st Lieutenant James Calhoun
                  2nd Lieutenant Henry M. Harrington
    Company E: 1st Lieutenant Thomas W. McDougall
    Company F: Captain George W. Yates
    Company G: 1st Lieutenant Donald McIntosh
                  2nd Lieutenant George D. Wallace
    Company H: Brevet Colonel Frederick W. Benteen
                  1st Lieutenant Frank M. Gibson
    Company K: Captain Owen Hale
                  1st Lieutenant Edward S. Godfrey
    Company L: Brevet Lieutenant Colonel Thomas W. Custer
    Company M: Captain Thomas H. French
                  1st Lieutenant Edward G. Mathey

Guides
    Louis Agard
    Boston Custer
    Charles Reynolds

Trainmaster (Wagonmaster)
    Michael Smith

Chief Packer
    J. C. Wagoner

Post Trader (Sutler)
    John W. Smith

Photographer
    William H. Illingworth

Correspondents
    William Eleroy Curtis, Chicago *Inter-Ocean*
    Samuel J. Barrows, New York *Tribune*
    Nathan H. Knappen, Bismarck, D.T., *Tribune*

Miners
    Horatio Nelson Ross
    William McKay

Scientists
    George Bird Grinnell
    Newton H. Winchell
    A. B. Donaldson
    Luther North

Index